# PORTRAITS
# OF HEROES
## DERBYSHIRE FIGHTER PILOTS
## IN THE SECOND WORLD WAR

# PORTRAITS OF HEROES
## DERBYSHIRE FIGHTER PILOTS IN THE SECOND WORLD WAR

BARRY M. MARSDEN

AMBERLEY

*Dedicated to all Derbyshire aircrew
who flew and fought in both world wars*

First published 2011

Amberley Publishing
Cirencester Road, Chalford,
Stroud, Gloucestershire GL6 8PE

www.amberleybooks.com

British Library Cataloguing in Publication Data.
A catalogue record for this book is available from the British Library.

ISBN 978-1-4456-0271-4

Typeset in 10pt on 12pt Sabon.
Typesetting and Origination by Amberley Publishing.
Printed in the UK.

# CONTENTS

# Acknowledgements

In preparing this book I would like to acknowledge the following for their help in providing photographs and information on the pilots whose combat careers form the basis of this work: John Anderson; Harry Baker; Rita Beddington; William Blackadder; Henry Boot; Audrey Burdekin; Peter Cornwell; Vera Davis; David Denchfield; David Drake-Feary; John Flinders; Norman Fryer; Alan Glover; Grub Street Publications; Marjorie Hancock; Sydney Hanson; Dulcie Henstock; Mike Hopkins; Trudi Humberstone; Jean Jackson; the *Kent Messenger*; Alan Mellor; Vera Musson; Sallie Ratledge; Bill Rolls; Philip Sanders; Andrew Saunders; Richard Shepley; Nos 1 and 609 Squadron Archives; Pauline Sturdy; Joan van Schaick; Freda Vickerstaffe; Donald Wilson; Johnathan Woolley.

# Photographs

While the majority of the photographs used in this work have been provided by the relatives and friends of the pilots concerned, the origins of others used are varied and often obscure, and some come from organisations and agencies no longer in existence. Any infringement of copyright is unintentional, and will be gladly rectified in future editions of the book.

# Introduction

This book is a belated companion to my *Derbyshire Fighter Aces of World War Two*, published by Tempus in 2004. The new book records the Air Force careers of thirty-three single-seat fighter pilots who hailed from my native county of Derbyshire and is the result of some twenty-five years of careful research. I feel it to be reasonably exhaustive, although the odd aviator may have escaped the net, and one individual I sought to interview long ago had no wish to participate in my investigations.

This present work is intended mainly as a photographic record. It includes almost 300 images, many of them collected from the families of the airmen themselves. They are precious relics of the many brave men who sacrificed their lives to protect their country.

Derbyshire fighter pilots fought throughout the war, from 1939 until 1945. They made their mark in the Battle of Britain, flew sweeps over Occupied Europe in 1941 and operated over Syria, North Africa, Malta, Sicily, Italy and Greece. They combated Focke-Wulf Condors over the Atlantic and the Japanese over the Timor Sea, and took part in the aerial campaigns over the Continent between 1943 and Germany's final defeat. I hope this sincere tribute will ensure that the sacrifices of Derbyshire's worthy aviators are not entirely lost to mind.

Barry M. Marsden
Eldwick
November 2010

# Abbreviations

| | |
|---|---|
| AACU | Anti-Aircraft Co-operation Unit |
| AAF | Auxiliary Air Force |
| ADU | Aircraft Delivery Unit |
| AFC | Air Force Cross |
| AFS | Advanced Flying School |
| AFDU | Air Fighting Development Unit |
| AFU | Advanced Fighting Unit |
| ALG | Advanced Landing Ground |
| ANZAC | Australia and New Zealand Army Corps |
| ASR | Air Sea Rescue |
| BFTS | British Flying Training School |
| CB | Companion of the Bath |
| CFI | Chief Flying Instructor |
| CFS | Central Flying School |
| CGI | Chief Ground Instructor |
| CGS | Central Gunnery School |
| CO | Commanding Officer |
| DCM | Distinguished Conduct Medal |
| DFC | Distinguished Flying Cross |
| DFM | Distinguished Flying Medal |
| DSO | Distinguished Service Order |
| EFS | Elementary Flying School |
| EFTS | Elementary Flying Training School |
| E&RFTS | Elementary & Reserve Flying Training School |
| FIS | Flying Instructors' School |
| FTS | Flying Training School |
| HQ | Headquarters |
| ITW | Initial Training Wing |
| MM | Military Medal |

| | |
|---|---|
| MOD | Ministry of Defence |
| MSFU | Merchant Ship Fighter Unit |
| NCO | Non-Commissioned Officer |
| OBE | Order of the British Empire |
| OC | Officer Commanding |
| OFU | Overseas Flying Unit |
| OTU | Operational Training Unit |
| POW | Prisoner of War |
| PRC | Personnel Reception Centre |
| RAF | Royal Air Force |
| RAFVR | Royal Air Force Volunteer Reserve |
| RCAF | Royal Canadian Air Force |
| RFC | Royal Flying Corps |
| RFS | Reserve Flying School |
| RT | Radio Telephone |
| SFTS | Service Flying Training School |
| SHAPE | Supreme Headquarters Allied Powers in Europe |
| TAF | Tactical Air Force |
| TEU | Tactical Exercise Unit |
| USAAC | United States Army Air Corps |
| WT | Wireless Telegraphy |

# Victories Claimed by Derbyshire Fighter Pilots Flying Single-Seat Fighters

| Pilot | Destroyed | Shared destroyed | Probable | Damaged |
|---|---|---|---|---|
| Sqn Ldr A. V. Clowes | 8 | 3 | 3 | 4 |
| Flt Lt N. Taylor | 8 | 2 | 1 | 3 |
| Air Cdre P. J. Sanders | 6 | – | 3 | – |
| Sgt A. N. Feary | 5 | 1 | 1 | 5 |
| Sqn Ldr J. L. Flinders | 5 | 1 | – | 1 |
| Sqn Ldr H. C. Baker | 4 | 2 | – | 5 |
| Sgt W. B. Higgins | 4 | 1 | – | 1 |
| Sqn Ldr N. V. Glew | 3 + 1 grd | 3 | 2 | 7 + 2 grd |
| PO F. Mellor | 2 | 3 | 1 | 2 |
| Wg Cdr F. G. Woolley | 4 | – | 1 | 1 |
| PO F. R. Walker-Smith | 3 | 1 | – | – |
| Flt Lt J. E. van Schaick | 2 | – | 2 | 2 |
| Flt Lt C. E. Bowen | 2 | 2 | – | 3 |
| PO D. C. Shepley | 2 | – | – | 1 |
| Flt Lt J. S. Anderson | 1 | 2 | – | 1 |
| Sqn Ldr L. F. Henstock | – | 3 | 1 | 3 |
| PO W. L. Davis | 1 | – | 1 | 1 |
| PO J. A. Wain | 1 | – | – | 3 |
| Flt Lt F. Meakin | – | 1 | – | – |
| PO C. W. J. Fearn | – | – | – | 3 |
| *Total* | 61 | 25 | 16 | 46 |

# The Derby Volunteer Reservists

The RAFVR was formed in July 1936 to provide aircrew to supplement the AAF, which had been formed in 1925 by the local Territorial Associations. Initially, the VR was composed of civilians recruited from the Reserve Flying Schools that used reserve RAF officers as tutors. Recruits were confined to men of between eighteen and twenty-five years of age who were accepted for part-time training as pilots, observers and wireless operators – the object being to provide a reserve pool of aircrew for use in the event of war. By September 1939, the organisation comprised some 6,500 pilots, 1,600 observers and 2,000 wireless operators.

In the spring of 1939, twenty-nine promising RAF Volunteer Reservists were given the opportunity to undertake a two-month course in *ab initio* flight training at No. 11 E&RFTS at Prestwick, Ayr. Among the line-up were four Derby reservists – Norman Glew (back row third from left), Richard Glover (sixth from left), Norman Taylor (second from right) and Eric Wardel-Knight (middle row, third from right). Only Norman Taylor survived the war.

On 1 September 1939, some 250 Derby VRs posed for a group photograph at Highfield, the VR HQ in Derby. Sitting on the far right of the back row is Sergeant Pilot Alan Feary, the first of the local reservists to gain his 'wings'. To his right are Sergeants Wardel-Knight, Glew and Glover. At the bottom left is 'Bill' Davis. All the pilots except Wardel-Knight were drafted onto fighters.

In another part of the photograph were the other early trainees. From left to right (back row) they include Frank Walker-Smith, also sporting his flying badge, Harold Hunt, Denis Crowley-Milling (later Air Marshal Sir Denis), and Tony Evershed.

The advanced trainee section was photographed the same day, together with Wing Commander Clifford A. B. Wilcock, commandant of the Derby VR (seated second from left). Also in the shot are, from left, Evershed, Davis, Glover and Wardel-Knight. Walker-Smith is seated bottom right.

Six of the original VRs line up in the Highfield garden. From left to right they include Hunt, Walker-Smith, Glew, Crowley-Milling, Glover and Wardel-Knight. Two of the six were dead before the end of 1940.

The six would-be aviators indulge in some strenuous tomfoolery; Hunt is hoisted on the others' shoulders. Hunt later became a highly decorated Beaufighter pilot in the Far East, winning the DSO, the DFC and later the AFC. He was drowned in 1965 attempting to rescue a fellow yachtsman.

# Derbyshire Presentation Spitfires

The idea of raising funds to buy an aeroplane for the RAF was the brainchild of Lord Beaverbrook, the dynamic Minister of Aircraft Production. Capital was provided from a variety of sources, including donations from individuals, families, cities, towns, counties, factories, and collieries, as well as from British colonies and nominally neutral countries. The glamour of the Spitfire fighter made it a favourite choice, and many hundreds of these iconic aircraft were purchased for the RAF during the Second World War.

The first Derbyshire Presentation Spitfire was *The Derby Ram* (X4994), a Mk I seen here before its allocation to a squadron. First flown on 13 March 1941, it served throughout the war and was struck off charge in April 1945.

*Bolsover 1* (R7261) was one of two fighters purchased by the small mining town. A Mk Vb, it first flew on 26 March 1941 and like the *Derby Ram* it survived the war, and was sold for scrapping in September 1945. *Bolsover 11* (R7276), another Mk V, served with 91 Squadron as DL-Z and crashed into the sea on 9 September 1941, incurring the loss of the pilot.

*Buxton* (P8660), a Mk IIb, first flew in May 1941 and served until it was written off after a ground collision. The aircraft is shown here after allotment to 54 Squadron as KL-P. The pilot is a Canadian, Sergeant Eric Pook. 'Hope' is not the Derbyshire township near Buxton, but the name of Pook's pet turtle!

*Shepley* (W3649) was a Mk Vb purchased with donations to the Shepley family of Holmesfield. It lost three siblings to enemy action in the first year of the war. It first flew on 1 August 1941, and became the personal mount of Group Captain F. V. Beamish, station commander of the Kenley Wing. Coded FV-B, it was shot down over the Channel on 28 March 1942, incurring the loss of its pilot.

# Flight Lieutenant
# John Stuart Anderson AE

John Anderson was born in Spondon, Derby, on 9 November 1920 of Franco-Scottish parents. His father was a chemist working for British Celanese. He joined the Derby RAFVR in January 1938 and on the outbreak of war attended 4 ITW Bexhill, 5 EFTS Hanworth and 5 SFTS Sealand before moving to 7 OTU Hawarden. He then joined 152 Squadron at Warmwell in September 1940, moved the next month to 234 Squadron, and returned to 152 in November. He undertook no Battle of Britain sorties, but had a chequered time between October and the following June, which involved three 'incidents': landing 'wheels up', hitting an anti-glider post while landing at the wrong airfield, and again landing with his undercarriage retracted. In June 1941 he was posted to 91 Squadron, where he saw no action, and in October he was sent to the Middle East, where he joined 73 OTU in Aden. After a spell in transit camps and hospital, Anderson was posted to 33 (Hurricane) Squadron in March 1942, followed by a further posting in August to 145 Squadron on Spitfires. By then a flight sergeant, he was promoted to warrant officer, and was commissioned in January 1943. While with the squadron he claimed a Macchi 202 (shot down), shared an Me 109E and a Junkers 88, and damaged two further Me 109s. His tour completed, he was posted in June 1943 to 71 OTU at Ismailia as an instructor. In May 1944 he joined 94 (Spitfire) Squadron in the Eastern Mediterranean, and in October he moved to Kalamaki, Greece, taking part in operations against Communist insurgents and the retreating Germans, sharing a Heinkel 111 destroyed on the ground. In March 1945, he was posted to 253 Squadron with the Balkan Air Force in Italy, but in May he was repatriated to England, where he was released from service in October. He subsequently worked for Rolls-Royce in the purchasing department, and now lives in retirement in Derby.

*Portraits of Heroes*

*Above left:* John Anderson in Ismaïlia, in 1943.

*Above right:* John, in flying kit, in front of Spitfire 11a UM-C at Warmwell in late 1940. The sky spinner and black underside to the port wing and undercarriage fairing date the image to between November 1940 and April 1941.

John is pictured here in the cockpit of UM-C. The shot picks out the armoured windscreen and rear-view mirror.

*Right:* John, on the right, is seen with Sergeant Bill Rudd (on the left) and Sergeant Howard Marsh at RAF Portreath, Cornwall, in the spring of 1941.

*Below:* Anderson poses in the 'office' of Presentation Spitfire Vb W3405 (DL-N) *Monmouth, Chepstow and Forest of Dean*, 91 Squadron, in the summer of 1941. The image picks out the details of cockpit and canopy.

Flying a tropicalised Hurricane IIb, John is here seen patrolling the Western Desert while serving with 33 Squadron in the summer of 1942. Note the drag-inducing Vokes air filter clearly visible beneath the nose of the aeroplane.

A tropicalised Spitfire Vb of John's unit, 145 Squadron, was the first Spitfire element to serve in North Africa. Again note how the Vokes filter spoils the clean lines of the aircraft's nose.

# Squadron Leader
# Henry Collingham Baker

Harry 'Butch' Baker was born in Clowne (a subject of wry amusement to him throughout his life) in May 1920, the son of a local headmaster. He joined the RAF on a short-service commission in 1938, training at 9 EFTS Ansty, Uxbridge, and 7 FTS Hullavington. He was posted to 1 Electrical and Wireless School at Cranwell as a staff pilot in May 1939. In September he joined 616 Squadron before attending 55 OTU in Aston Down. In November he moved to 19 (Spitfire) Squadron and saw action over Dunkirk, shooting down an Me 110 and damaging a second. He was hospitalised in June 1940 after a car accident, and was posted to 41 Squadron in late August. While with this unit, he claimed an Me 109E, a share in a Heinkel 111, and damage to a second Heinkel. He was also forced to crash-land his Spitfire on one occasion, after combat with 109s. In October he moved to 421 Flight, where he destroyed two Me 109Es, had a share in a third, and damaged two more. In January 1941, he was posted to 74 Squadron, claiming an Me 109F while serving with this unit. In late July he became an instructor with 52 OTU at Debden and 5 OTU at Aston Down, where a broken ankle necessitated a further spell in hospital. On recovery he was sent to the Middle East, where he joined 127 Squadron in May 1942 as a flight lieutenant, and shared a tent with Ian Smith, future prime minister of Southern Rhodesia. In September he was posted to Malta as CO of 229 Squadron, where he damaged two Me 109Fs in combat. After a period of sickness he returned to England in December as OC Tactical Training at HQ Northern Ireland. In April 1943 he moved to 55 OTU, Annan, before a spell in Gibraltar, ferrying Hurricanes to Cairo. His final operational tour was as a supernumerary flight lieutenant with 118 Squadron. In 1944 he spent time as a ferry pilot at Croydon, took an instructor's course at CFS Montrose, and had a spell as CFI at Wrexham. In January 1945 he became CGI at 17 FTS Cranwell. He ended his RAF career at Kimbolton in charge of the Recruits' Training Wing. Demobilised in early 1946, Harry tried his hand at tea planting in Ceylon, followed by a spell with

Peru State Railways, before joining a Grimsby company operating cargo vessels. His expertise led to several directorships and an accolade as 'one of Humberside's leading shipping men' before his retirement in the 1980s. As with other Derbyshire-born 'aces', the lack of a suitable decoration was a slur on a dedicated fighting airman.

A youthful Harry 'Butch' Baker as a pilot officer in early 1940.

*Right:* Harry at his wedding to Betty Todd at Gainsborough Church in October 1940. He had to postpone his nuptials, scheduled for 15 September, for obvious reasons.

*Below:* Harry, second from right, poses in front of Presentation Spitfire 11a P8388 (ZP-W) *Black Vanities* with fellow pilots of 74 Squadron, in the spring of 1941. While piloting this aircraft, he shot down an Me 109F on 26 May.

# Flight Lieutenant Charles Earle Bowen

Charles 'Chatty' Bowen was born in Chapel-en-le-Frith on 2 February 1916, of Anglo-Spanish parents; his father was a shipping agent. He joined the RAF on a short service commission in 1936, training at the de Havilland factory airfield at Hatfield, and at 9 FTS Ansty. In October 1937 he was posted to 77 Squadron at Honington to fly Vickers Wellesley bombers, but in May 1938 he was transferred to 10 FTS Tern Hill as an instructor. In July he was appointed aide-de-camp to Air Marshal Sir Arthur Longmore, C-in-C Transport Command, and remained in post until September 1939, when his request to transfer to operational flying was granted. After short stays with 145 and 615 squadrons, he moved to 607, based in France, in December. 607 was swapping its outmoded Gladiators for Hurricanes, and when the Germans launched their Blitzkreig in May 1940, he claimed a share in a Heinkel 111 and damaged a second. After withdrawing to England, the unit was in action over the Tyne and Bowen claimed a destroyed Heinkel 111. Promoted to flight lieutenant in early September, he was again in action when the squadron moved south, claiming a destroyed Dornier 17Z, plus a share in a Me 110 and damage to a Junkers 88 and a Me 110. He was shot down over the Isle of Wight on 26 September and baled out safely, but on 1 October he was lost in combat with Me 110s in the same locality. His name is recorded on the Runnymede Memorial.

*Right:* 'Chatty' Bowen appears here early in 1940 while stationed in France with 607 Squadron.

*Below:* 'Chatty' relaxes as he catches up with his correspondence in the flight hut at Tangmere, September 1940.

'Chatty', wearing a prized German *Schwimmvest*, discusses tactics with friend and fellow-pilot, the Pole Franciszek Surma.

# Flight Sergeant Henry Shaw Brown

Harry Brown was born in Derby on 18 May 1921. He was a Rolls-Royce apprentice before the war, joined the RAFVR in June 1941 and trained in Canada. He served with 175 Squadron for a short period in mid-1943 before transferring to 174. Both units operated Typhoon fighter bombers. On 18 February 1944, Harry was on an operational flight over France and was last seen some 20 miles south-east of Beachy Head in deteriorating weather, apparently climbing to clear a snowstorm. He failed to return, and his body was never recovered. His name appears on the Runnymede Memorial.

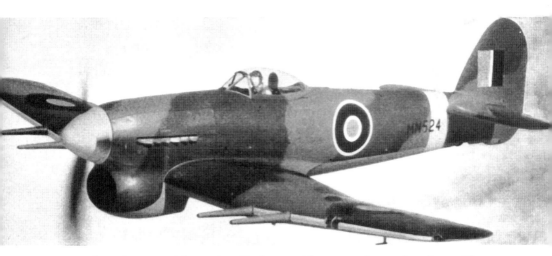

Harry flew the powerful Hawker Typhoon with 174 and 175 Squadrons. The fighter packed a fearsome punch with its four 20 mm cannon, plus bombs or 6-inch rockets.

Harry Brown as a cadet – as shown by the white flash on his forage cap.

# Squadron Leader
# Arthur Victor Clowes
# DFC DFM

Arthur 'Darky' Clowes was born in New Sawley on 12 August 1912, and was brought up by his grandparents, his father having been killed serving with the Sherwood Foresters in 1917 (his mother had subsequently decamped to Australia with an ANZAC private). He was determined to have a career in the RAF and at the age of sixteen he enlisted as an aircraft apprentice at 4 Wing, Halton. Remustering as a fitter in 1936, he was chosen for pilot training and joined 6 FTS Netheravon, soloing that September. He was promoted to sergeant pilot and posted to 1 Squadron at Tangmere, flying Hawker Furies. The unit went to France in September 1939 and in an early air battle he shot down a Heinkel 111, despite having had part of his Hurricane's tail sliced off in a collision with a French Curtiss 75A Hawk. He pulled off a skilful forced landing back at base, despite the damage to his fighter. He shared in the destruction of an Me 110 at the end of March 1940, and when the Germans launched their attack in May he destroyed two Me 109Es, plus a Junkers 87 and an Me 110, shared a Heinkel 111, and damaged another Me 109 in the subsequent Battle of France. He was awarded a DFM and a Mention in Despatches, and was commissioned in September. During the Battle of Britain, still with 1 Squadron, he shot down two Heinkel 111s, an Me 110, and shared a Dornier 215. In addition he claimed no less than three 'probables' – two Dornier 17Zs, and an Me 110 – and damaged two further Heinkels and another Me 110. Arthur was awarded a DFC in May 1941. Rested from operations, he went to 56 OTU at Heston as an instructor, returning to operations in December as CO 79 Squadron. When this unit was sent to the Far East, he undertook several staff appointments before joining 601 Squadron in the Western Desert, leading them for three months before becoming senior controller of Sector Operations at Middle East HQ. He later led 94 Squadron in the Eastern Mediterranean before returning to further HQ and administrative duties. Unfortunately, he lost his left eye in a bout of high spirits in the mess, an accident that put paid to his flying career and left him grounded in a series of administrative posts. Granted a permanent commission, Arthur was seconded to the Air Ministry after the war, and his last posting was to HQ Technical Training Command at Brampton Grange, Huntingdon. Tragically he contracted cancer of the liver and died in the RAF Hospital, Ely, on 7 December 1949, at the age of thirty-seven. He is buried in the churchyard of St Mary Magdalen, Brampton.

*Above left:* 'Darky' Clowes in late 1939 when he was a sergeant with No. 1 Squadron.

*Above right:* Airman Clowes, aged sixteen, poses proudly for this studio portrait taken on his joining the RAF in January 1929.

Arthur, standing second from the right, is shown with the cup-winning RAF football team in the early 1930s. Air Commodore Bonham-Carter sits in the centre, flanked on his right by the formidable-looking Warrant Officer Cavill.

Trainee pilot Arthur Clowes flies his first solo in an Avro Cadet in the autumn of 1936.

'Darky' is flying somewhere amid this stepped-up echelon of No. 1's sleek and elegant Hawker Furies.

Arthur shows off his beloved Riley convertible sometime in the late 1930s. The conveyance is notable for its split windscreen and battery of headlights.

No. 1 Squadron pilots and groundcrew line up by their hastily camouflaged Furies at Tangmere at the time of the Munich crisis. 'Darky', in customary white overalls, stands behind the squadron hound; on his right is Philip Sanders, who was also serving with the unit at this time.

Squadron Leader 'Bull' Halahan, the unit's charismatic commander, plays with an MG 15 machine gun liberated from a shot-down Dornier 17. Paul Richey, who later wrote the bestseller *Fighter Pilot*, points out the salient features of the weapon, while Arthur looks on with interest.

Boys will be boys. Richey tries his hand at sighting the unfamiliar trophy, flanked by Arthur on his right, and Flight Commander 'Johnny' Walker on his left.

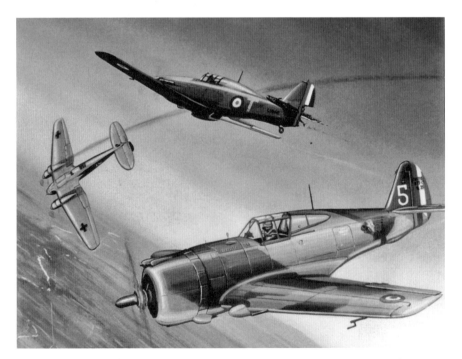

On 23 November 1939, Arthur's Hurricane was hit by an impatient French Curtiss Hawk 75A while he was attacking a Heinkel 111 over Saarbrucken. The impact sheared off most of his rudder, an incident shown in this reconstruction.

*Right:* A relieved-looking 'Darky' shows off his damaged fighter L1842 (JX-T), which he force-landed with great skill after the French fighter had carved off much of his tail unit during his attack on the Heinkel.

*Below:* Arthur enters the cockpit of his stalwart Hurricane P3395 (JX-B), snug in its blast pen at Collyweston in the autumn of 1940. Note the scuffed paintwork under the cockpit, and the small square anti-gas panel on the wing.

*Above:* 'Darky', in his trademark white overalls, stands by the nose of P3395, which bears his personal emblem, a fearsome striped wasp. Each black stripe represented a confirmed 'kill'.

*Left:* A charcoal portrait of Flight Lieutenant Clowes DFM, drawn by the war artist Cuthbert Orde on 22 February 1941.

No. 1 Squadron's pilots, including a number of foreign flyers, line up at Wittering in November 1940. Arthur, top left, nurses the squadron dog; CO 'Hilly' Brown is second from left, bottom row.

'Home is the hunter.' Squadron Leader Clowes' flag-draped coffin is laid to rest with full military honours in St Mary Magdalene churchyard, Brampton, Huntingdon, on 10 December 1949.

*Left:* The simple
marble cross marks
the last resting place
of Derbyshire's
foremost fighter ace
of the Second World
War.

*Below:* A Hurricane
Mk IV from
the Birmingham
Museum of Science
and Industry
masquerades as
Darky's P3395
on Horse Guards
Parade on
15 September
1990, the fiftieth
anniversary of the
Battle of Britain.

# Flying Officer
# William Lance Davis

Bill Davis was born in Spondon on 19 March 1919, the son of a hosiery factory owner. He joined the Derby VR in 1938, and when war broke out he was posted to 1 ITW at Cambridge, from whence he progressed to 5 FTS Sealand in January 1940, followed by 6 OTU Sutton Bridge in July. He joined 249 Squadron at the beginning of August, where his CO, Tom Neil, described him as 'the charming Sergeant Davis who reminded me so much of P. G. Wodehouse's Bertie Wooster'. During September, Bill destroyed a Junkers 88, claimed an Me 109E probable, and damaged a Dornier 17Z. His Hurricane was shot down on 11 September, but he baled out near Benedon, slightly wounded. Bill was commissioned in February 1941, but only two days later he was shot down into the English Channel by Me 109Es during a sweep on 10 February. Taken prisoner, he spent the rest of the war as a POW, despite serious damage to his leg. In a card sent from Stalag IX-E in June 1942 to his friend Norman Glew, he confessed, 'God, it's boring over here, you can have no idea how much I miss my flying!!' He added, 'My leg is still pretty unserviceable, which is a hell of a bind!' After the war he remained in the family hosiery business, and died at Hinckley on 30 March 1984.

Sergeant 'Bill' Davis while serving with the Derby RAFVR.

In this line-up of personnel at No. 1 ITW, Cambridge, taken in late 1939, Bill can be seen second from right, top row.

Bill's tall figure can be seen on the left as he poses with fellow trainees in Cambridge during the bitter winter of 1939–40.

Bill takes the wheel of his basic-looking hotrod. The bonnet is strapped down, perhaps to prevent the engine escaping. Alongside is the imperturbable presence of his brother James, an officer in the Royal Marines.

# Warrant Officer
# David Denchfield

'Dave' Denchfield was born on 2 November 1919 at Eckington, although he moved to Hemel Hempstead, where he worked as a clerk. He joined the RAFVR at Luton in May 1939 and did his elementary flying at 29 E&RFTS. After the outbreak of war he was posted to 4 ITW at Bexhill, and progressed to 15 EFTS Redhill in late April 1940. He moved to 15 FTS Brize Norton in June, then to 15 AFS Chipping Norton in August. He did his final training at 7 OTU Hawarden and was posted to 610 Squadron on 7 October as a sergeant pilot. On a Blenheim escort to St Omer on 2 February 1941, Dave was acting as 'weaver' to the squadron when his Spitfire was hit, and he was forced to bale out near Wizernes Airfield. It appears he was the fortieth victim of Walter Oesau of JG 3, whose silver cigarette case he duly autographed. He remained a POW until his release on 1 May 1945 as a warrant officer. He joined A. V. Roe as a design draughtsman and rejoined the RAFVR in 1949 at 6 RFS Sywell. He remained with the unit until its disbandment in 1953. He retired from employment with British Aerospace in 1984.

'Dave' Denchfield in an image dating from his post-war RAF service.

Dave was shot down on 5 February 1941 while escorting Blenheims to St Omer with Spitfire N3249 (DW-P). He baled out and is seen here immediately after capture. He spent the rest of the war as a POW.

# Pilot Officer Sydney John Anthony Evershed

Tony Evershed was born in Lullington in August 1916. His grandfather, Sir Herbert Evershed, captained the Derbyshire County Cricket XI in the 1890s, and his own short life was both varied and exciting. In 1934 he volunteered for a cadetship on the world cruise of Alan Villiers' sailing ship the *Joseph Conrad*. She was the last full-rigged vessel to circumnavigate the world under sail, and Evershed was promoted cadet captain by her noted skipper. In 1938 he joined the Derby VR, progressing from Burnaston through the various stages of pilot training, which culminated at 5 OTU Aston Down. As an acting pilot officer, he was posted to 54 Squadron at Rochford, commanded by Squadron Leader 'Al' Deere. Unfortunately, Tony's first operational mission was his last. On 9 July, his flight was ordered to intercept a Heinkel 59 floatplane, which was overflying a convoy near the Goodwin Sands. Tony's Yellow Section, led by Deere, was tasked with holding off the escorting Me 109s while Red Section forced down the Heinkel. All three Yellow Section Spitfires were lost. Deere shot down a 109 and collided with a second. He managed to force-land at Manston. Tony's fighter was swallowed up by the English Channel somewhere south of Dover, and he died one day before the 'official' start of the Battle of Britain. His family were thus denied the bar awarded for service in this vital conflict. Deere later wrote of him, 'He was one of the brightest of the new boys. I had high hopes of him turning into a good section leader.' He is commemorated on the Runnymede Memorial, and his erstwhile captain, Villiers, later described him as 'A stalwart on a royal yard in a breeze of wind, a tower of strength on a weather reef bearing, a sure master of the bucking wheel in many a down south gale; aye, and a stalwart at the controls of a Spitfire until the end, that was Tony Evershed. A fine boy, and a fine young man.'

Tony Evershed serving with the Derby RAFVR.

# Flight Lieutenant
# Charles W. J. Fearn

Much of Charles Fearn's service career remains obscure, but we know that he was born in Derby, and after training was posted to 601 Squadron AAF, just too late to participate in the Battle of Britain. In May 1941, he damaged a Me 109F over the English Channel, but was himself wounded in the action and crash-landed in Manston. 1942 found him at the Practice Flight, Setif, Algeria, from which he was posted to 93 Squadron in November, and was occupied mainly in ground-attack duties. He moved to 243 Squadron in March 1943, and damaged two Me 109Fs on one day. On 24 April he was shot down by enemy flak while attacking German transport, and was again wounded, finishing up at a hospital in Tunis. He was liberated when the Allies occupied the city, although it appears he had suffered a damaged or blinded eye. He was repatriated and apparently worked at Heathrow Airport after the war.

Although much of Charles Fearn's air force career is still obscure, his image has been caught here, just after the Battle of Britain, in this line-up of 601's pilots.

# Sergeant Pilot
# Alan Norman Feary

Alan Feary was born in Derby on 12 April 1912, the son of a horse inspector on the Midland Railway. He worked in Derby Borough's treasurer's department, and his leisure interests included amateur dramatics, sports and motor vehicles. He joined the RAFVR in 1936, becoming the first of the Derby VRs to gain his 'wings'. With the outbreak of war he was posted to 9 FTS Hullavington, followed by 5 OTU at Aston Down in April 1940. After a short period with 600 Squadron AAF as a sergeant pilot, he joined 609 Squadron AAF at Northolt in June. The unit moved to Middle Wallop in early July, and during the ensuing Battle of Britain, he destroyed an Me 109E, two Me 110s, a Junkers 87 and a Junkers 88, and shared a further Ju 88. In claiming the last victim, his two companion pilots were both shot down by the Junkers' rear gunner; one baled out, the other crash-landed, and Alan was the only member of the flight to return to base. He also claimed a probable Me 109E, which was almost certainly destroyed, and damaged five more enemy aircraft. On 7 October, he was killed baling out of his Spitfire near Warmwell at too low a height after combat with Me 109s. He was buried in the churchyard of Holy Trinity, Warmwell. That he received no decoration for his distinguished service remains a disgrace.

*Left:* A 1939 studio portrait of Sergeant Pilot Alan Feary.

*Below:* Alan, in white overalls, discusses the day's activities at Burnaston Airfield with fellow trainees, including Denis Crowley-Milling (second left) and Harold Hunt (third left). Note the Tiger Moth and Magister elementary trainers on the left, and the smoke wind-direction marker.

Hawker Audax K3707 on the left, and Hind K5547 alongside, line up at Burnaston in the spring of 1939. The latter is warming up for take-off. Feary is on the right, just in front of the balding civilian type.

Alan pilots Hind 5547 above the south Derbyshire countryside as he builds up his pre-war flying hours.

Alan poses in flying gear at Burnaston in the summer of 1939 with the now-demolished Burnaston House behind him. Rather poignantly, the whole airport area is now covered by the Derby Toyota car factory.

On 13 August 1940, 609 Squadron claimed thirteen enemy aircraft in action over Lyme Bay, Dorset. Here the jubilant pilots line up at Warmwell after the successful action. Alan stands third from right, and CO Darley is fifth from right. David Crook, who later wrote *Spitfire Pilot*, is kneeling centre front. The basic facilities of the forward base are clearly evident.

*Right:* The squadron scoreboard for the lucky 13 August shows that nearly every pilot claimed something on that memorable day.

*Below:* Hangar 5 at Middle Wallop was devastated by bombs from a Junkers 88 on 14 August. The raider was subsequently shot down by Feary. Here, the destruction of the huge building is clearly evident. The roof is blasted to matchwood and the huge doors are lying flat.

One hangar door still remained intact after the blasts, although the structure around it was severely damaged.

In this shot the 13-ton hangar doors lie flattened on the right, crushing the three brave airmen who were desperately trying to close them. Between them and the pitted wall, a 604 Squadron Blenheim fighter can just be seen.

Three Spitfires of 609 Squadron were smashed by the German bombs inside the hangar. The remains of two of the machines are clearly visible.

Keith Bruce's painting shows Alan's Spitfire L1065 (PR-E) pursuing the Junkers 88 over Boscombe Down, where he shot it down to register his third 'kill'.

The shattered wreckage of the LG1 raider lies strewn across the down as juvenile souvenir hunters sift for mementoes. An airman, apparently wearing Luftwaffe goggles, poses behind a battered wing.

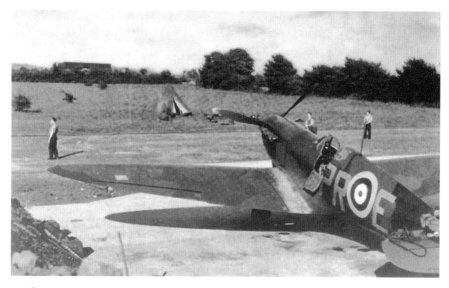

Spitfire L1065 stands ready in its pen at Wallop with the pilot's parachute and helmet at hand on the port tailplane. Note the scuffed, bare metal along the wing root, and the anti-gas panel near the wingtip. Alan shot down two enemy aircraft while flying this machine.

Alan dictates a combat report to Flying Officer Mackay, 609's intelligence officer, after an operational sortie.

Alan stands in thoughtful mood in an off-duty moment at Wallop. The tea drinker is probably Polish fellow ace Tadeusz Nowierski.

*Left:* Alan's grave is situated in the military section of the churchyard at Holy Trinity, Warmwell.

*Below:* In 1987, Derby Industrial Museum dedicated a permanent memorial to Alan Feary, which was opened by the city's mayor. Here the author, left, and curator Brian Waters look over Alan's medals and other memorabilia, which rest on a Merlin engine of 1940 vintage.

# Squadron Leader
# John Layton Flinders

John 'Polly' Flinders was born in Chesterfield on 3 August 1917 and joined the RAF in January 1936. His *ab initio* training took place at the Bristol Flying School at Filton, followed by a spell at 3 FTS, Grantham. He was posted to 74 Squadron in December 1936 as a sergeant pilot, and remained with the unit until April 1940. While with 74 he shared in the destruction of a Dornier 17F reconnaissance aircraft in November 1939. He was commissioned, moved to 32 Squadron, and took part in sweeps over France in May–June 1940, shooting down an Me 109E and a Heinkel 111 and damaging a further Heinkel. On one occasion he was shot down by enemy flak, force-landed his Hurricane near Cap Griz Nez, and returned to England via Boulogne. When the Battle of Britain commenced, he claimed an Me 109E, whose pilot later presented him with his helmet and flying suit, and two Me 110s, both shot down in one engagement. In March 1941, he was posted to 55 OTU Aston Down, and soon after this he took instruction courses at Upavon and Hullavington. He moved to 2 FIS Montrose in 1943 and then took an Empire CFS course back at Hullavington, which was a precursor to his posting to CFS Trenton, Canada, where he gained 'exceptional' ratings both as a pilot and instructor. He was subsequently transferred to the RCAF at Trenton, and joined the Visiting Flight, where he assessed pupils and instructors. He returned to England in March 1945, left the service in November, and joined the Firestone Tyre Company, where he filled various sales executive positions. On retirement, he emigrated to Canada, where he died in July 1998. Again John seems to have been deemed unworthy of recognition, either for his 'ace' status, or for his outstanding work in wartime pilot instruction.

*Above left:* Pilot Officer John 'Polly' Flinders in 1940.

*Above right:* John, as a sergeant pilot with 74 Squadron, is standing in front of one of the unit's Gauntlet fighters in 1938.

John joined 32 Squadron in 1940, and after intensive operations over France and England, the unit was withdrawn to Acklington for rest. The photograph shows one section of the flight hut with Flight Lieutenant Peter Gardner (on the left) discussing the latest aircraft recognition sheets with the squadron intelligence officer. The NCO in the background is Flight Sergeant McCloughlin, a member of the squadron groundcrew. Note the portable radio and model aeroplanes on the central table.

Another part of the hut reveals pilots relaxing in the rather basic quarters. Aircraft posters flank a single discreet pin-up.

John as a squadron leader in Canada in 1943.

*Left:* In 1995, John
posed for this shot,
wearing the helmet
and flying suit
donated by
Lt Horst Marx,
whom he shot down
over Frant on 15
August 1940.

*Below:* The
32 Squadron
scoreboard, painted
on a Hurricane
wingtip and now
displayed at the RAF
Museum, Hendon.
The combat victories
of Flinders and
Burley Higgins are
recorded here.

# Squadron Leader
# Norman Vipan Glew

Born in Derby in November 1916, Norman 'Sticky' Glew, whose father was an officer in the Sherwood Foresters in the First World War and was later an auditor, trained as a dispensing chemist at Boots, although his ultimate objective was to fly with the RAF. He joined 30 E&RFTS at Derby and also notched up over 100 hours' flying at 11 E&RFTS, Prestwick, on a special course in the spring of 1939. With the outbreak of war Norman joined 1 ITW Cambridge, followed by a drafting to 3 FTS South Cerney in February 1940. In June, he was posted to 72 Squadron at Acklington, where he received tuition on fighter tactics on Harvards and Spitfires. In August he was lucky to survive when he crashed his aircraft while landing after a night flight, and in late August the unit moved south to take part in the Battle of Britain. During the ensuing conflict, Norman claimed two Me 110s destroyed, plus shares in an Me 109E and a Dornier 17Z, and a Junkers 88 and Me 109E probable. He also damaged three other enemy bombers, and was once forced to belly-land after damage in combat with Me 109s. In November, Norman was posted to 616 Squadron, but two weeks later he moved to 41, where he remained until May 1941, when, bored by inactivity, he volunteered for overseas service, joining 260 Squadron, which was bound for the Middle East. En route on the carrier HMS *Victorious*, progress was halted while the warship went in pursuit of the German battleship *Bismarck*. At Gibraltar, 260 transferred to the *Ark Royal*, from which it flew to Malta, and moved on to Palestine. In July, the unit was flying missions over Syria, attacking Vichy French airfields. Norman destroyed a Leo 257 on the ground, and damaged a Leo 451 and a Potez 63. In August he was commissioned, and remained with 260 until May 1942, serving with the unit in the Western Desert, where they exchanged their outmoded Hurricanes, first for Curtiss Tomahawks and subsequently for Kittihawks. While in North Africa, he destroyed a Junkers 87 and damaged two Me 109Fs before he was rested. He then undertook a variety of training and ferrying tasks before joining 229 Squadron in Malta and later Sicily. In

March 1944, he was promoted to command 1435 Squadron, stationed at
Brindisi in Italy. Here, on 17 May, he was killed when staging a mock dogfight
with a Spitfire; his Hurricane crashed near the airfield. Undecorated by his
country, he was buried near Brindisi, and he was subsequently moved to Bari
War Cemetery. 1435's adjutant wrote that 'his cheerful personality and ability
made him both a good comrade and an excellent leader'. Norman kept a fitful
diary from which useful information on his thoughts and wartime career can
be gleaned, and as a keen photographer he has left an invaluable archive for
aviation historians to study.

Norman Glew in the cockpit of a Spitfire Mk V in 1943. Note the crowbar clipped
to the inside of the cockpit door.

*Above left:* A determined-looking Norman prepares for a training flight in a Tiger Moth at No. 11 E&RFTS Ayr in late March 1939.

*Above right:* A group of would-be fliers pose at Prestwick, with Norman at the centre.

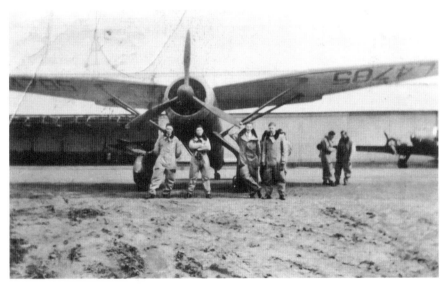

Fourth from the left, in flying kit, Norman forms part of a group in front of Lysander L4785 at Prestwick. Second from left is fellow Derbeian Eric Wardel-Knight.

Norman on ice. Marked by a cross, he takes time to relax with fellow trainees during the bitter winter of 1939–40 while serving with No. 1 ITW at Cambridge.

Norman, on the right, poses with friends at No. 3 FTS South Cerney, shortly after gaining his 'wings'. Left to right are sergeants Johnny White, Ted Hives (a fellow Derbeian), Johnny Gilders. The other pilot is unknown.

Intrepid airman Glew is about to take to the air after a posting to 72 Squadron at Acklington in the summer of 1940.

The 'Five Sprogs' at Acklington. The appellation was bestowed by their flight commander during squadron training. From left to right, back row: Sgt Gilders, PO Males, Sgt Rolls. Front row: Sgt White, Sgt Glew.

A relaxing moment at Acklington, with Norman and his inevitable pipe on the left and Johnny Gilders, a great friend, on the right.

Norman, proudly posed on the right, purchased this open-top 'hot rod' while at Acklington. Note the white-painted mudguards, deemed necessary for night-time blackout driving.

On 23 September 1940, Norman shared in the destruction of an Me 109E over Folkestone. A newspaper cameraman caught the crippled enemy warplane scraping over the Folkestone Mole before ditching, with Norman's Spitfire symbolically overflying its victim.

Norman and his Spitfire during the autumn of 1940, while the unit were stationed at Croydon.

In early November, Norman was posted to 616 Squadron at Kirton-in-Lindsey. In this posed view, sitting on the right and taken in the sergeants' mess, he contemplates his hand during a card game.

Norman only served for two weeks with 616. Here, in another obvious propaganda shot, he stands to the left of Flight Lieutenant Ken Holden as the pair chat to the squadron intelligence officer.

After a short spell with 41 Squadron, Norman volunteered for overseas service and joined 260 Squadron. The unit embarked on the carrier HMS *Victorious* at Scapa Flow in early May, bound for the Middle East. This doubtless illegal shot shows the carrier in company with the battleship HMS *King George V*.

The German warship *Bismarck* appeared in the Atlantic and Norman sailed with *Victorious* in pursuit. In this atmospheric photograph, taken on the flight deck, the carrier makes smoke. Note the battery of .50 calibre 'pom-poms' below the single funnel.

A Swordfish biplane takes off from *Victorious* during the search for the enemy battleship.

After the *Bismarck* had been sunk, the carrier and HMS *Ark Royal* refuelled in Britain and headed for Gibraltar. Here 260's Hurricanes are ranged on the deck of *Victorious*, while *Ark Royal* holds course on the right.

In early June, 260's fighters trans-shipped to *Ark Royal*. In this view, the tropicalised Hurricane 1s, equipped with fixed long-range tanks, await the order to fly to Malta. In the foreground is No. 17, whose serial number reads as Z456—.

On 14 June, escorted by Lockheed Hudson VX-K of 206 Squadron, 260's Hurricanes took off for Malta. Norman took this shot of the formation from the cockpit of his fighter.

*Above:* Squadron Leader 'Dickie' Mount's Hurricane 1 on its way to the island.

*Left:* Norman in a Tel Aviv street after the unit had arrived in Palestine.

A by-now-tropicalised Hurricane 1 of 260, wheels and flaps down, lands at El Bassa Airfield in Palestine in August 1941. Norman described the airstrip as being 'at the base of a damn great hill'.

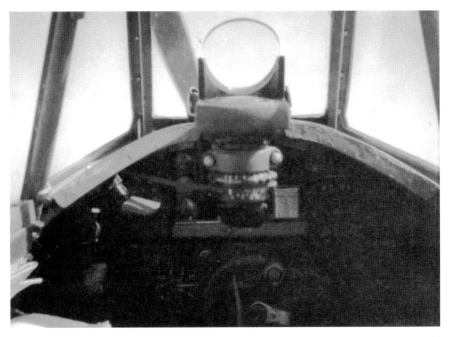

A pilot's eye-view of the cockpit of Norman's Hurricane, showing the Barr & Stroud GM2 reflector gunsight.

A smiling Norman sits in the cockpit of his Hurricane sometime during the unit's stay in Palestine.

Norman and his groundcrew pose by Hurricane 'E' in June 1941. He captioned this picture, 'A unit of the Middle East Air Force.'

The sad end of 'E' – pranged July 1941, courtesy of Pilot Officer Hanbury.

Another casualty was Hurricane Z4707 ('A') here being hauled upright after a nose-over.

*Above:* Norman in the 'office' of a Hawker Hart, used as a squadron hack during the unit's time in Palestine.

*Left:* One of the last images of Norman as a sergeant, taken in Tel Aviv shortly before his promotion to pilot officer in August 1941.

A more dishevelled shot of Norman, taken in the Western Desert, with tented accommodation visible in the background.

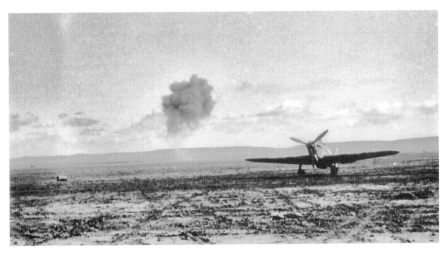

One of 260's Hurricanes ready for take-off under enemy fire in the Western Desert in late 1941.

German prisoners taken in the Eighth Army's push of late 1941, seen here at Msus, 260's base in December 1941–January 1942.

British forces retook Benghazi on 24 December 1941. Norman recorded this wrecked Ju 87 Stuka on the nearby Benina Airfield in January 1942.

Another view of the battered dive bomber with its distinctive spaghetti-type camouflage.

A smashed-up Messerschmitt 110 found on the same airfield.

This Junkers 88 was captured in a fairly good condition at Benina.

Italian aircraft were generally inferior in performance to those of the Luftwaffe. This derelict Breda 88 attack plane was obsolescent even at the start of the war. The Me 110 on page eighty-one is visible on the right of this picture.

Another derelict was this Heinkel 111 abandoned at Benina. The 1,000 lb bomb looks menacing enough on the ground.

This crashed and burned out Junkers 87 was claimed shot down by Norman near Benghazi in January 1942. An unexploded bomb lies on the left, near the starboard wing.

Near Benghazi, Norman examines a knocked-out German light tank, a victim of the see-sawing desert war.

British forces were pushed back in early 1942, and February found 260 at Martuba, south of Derna. Here the unit's pilots investigate a much-abused Junkers 87, with the skeleton of a burned-out hangar visible on the left.

Norman sitting on the Stuka wing, in his own words 'browned off with pongoes'. He is presumably contemplating the 8th Army's inability to hold on to its hard-won territory.

In February 1942, 260 exchanged its outmoded Hurricanes for American P40 Tomahawk Mk IIs. Norman is pictured here in front of one of the aggressive-looking new mounts, serial number AM419.

*Left:* Norman took a well-earned leave in Alexandria, a city he loved, in March 1942. Here he poses in unfamiliar blue in a relaxed mood.

*Below:* Norman stayed at the Hotel Cecil, and took this view of the lively cosmopolitan city from his room. It reveals wide boulevards serviced by a busy tramway system.

In March, 260 began re-equipping with Curtiss Kittihawks, and this fine shot shows one of the new warplanes that replaced the Tomahawks. Of interest are the 'MF' codes – a mystery since the unit's letters were usually 'HS'. By this time, the squadron was based at Gasr-el-Arid, near Gambut, Libya.

A squadron take-off by 260 in March 1942. Note the variant code on the second aircraft in line. It is partly obscured, but is obviously different to the norm.

Groundcrew work on the liquid-cooled Allison motor of one of the American fighters. Note the three .50 calibre Brownings in the port wing – capable of a devastating punch – and the back-up ring-and-bead sight in front of the windscreen.

Norman poses in the 'office' of his Kittihawk at Gasr-el-Arid. The second aircraft in line is a Tomahawk, suggesting the unit were operating both types at this time. Note the flatness of the surrounding landscape.

Norman's wingman, identified only as 'Sandy', is ready for action in March 1942. The photograph shows excellent detail of the sliding hood, the reflector gunsight and the padded headrest of the Curtiss fighter.

Taken from Norman's cockpit, this view shows a strafe on an unidentified target, with a fuel dump ablaze. The three Browning machine guns can be clearly seen in the fighter's starboard wing.

In an image taken shortly before his departure from the squadron, Norman waits the take-off call at the desert airfield in the cockpit of his Kittihawk.

Norman takes a ride in the rear seat of Harvard trainer AJ822. The aeroplane on the left is a Hurricane.

A neat shot of a Hurricane I with later 1942 roundels and fin flash. The fighter W9305 ('Q'), seems to have been sent to the Middle East and tropicalised in 1941. By 1942, it was probably in use as a squadron hack.

A superb aerial study of a Kittihawk 11a taken by Norman shows the fin fillet added to counter the take-off swing caused by the more powerful Allison engine. Note the auxiliary fuel tank, which suggests the aircraft was on a delivery flight.

The unexpected consequence of a lift. Norman hopped on this Blenheim IV to go on leave to Cairo, but the journey ended with a forced landing.

Another view of the crashed Blenheim suggests the port engine might have suffered a serious oil leak. Happily, no one was injured in the accident. Note the Fairey Albacores in the distance.

Norman took several images of crash-landings. Here, a Tomahawk has come to grief somewhere in the desert.

In this shot, a Beaufighter has come to earth, its airscrews buckled. The photograph shows clearly the open escape hatches to the cockpit and rear compartment.

In July 1942, Norman was taken off operations and put in charge of making an airstrip at Martuba, one of five constructed south of Derna. Here he proudly shows off his 'staff car' against a dreary backdrop of level sand.

The first aircraft to land at Norman's new airstrip was a tropicalised Spitfire Vb BP986 – shown here taxiing. This machine arrived in the Middle East in May, and was written off on 22 October after an operational sortie.

Another early visitor to Martuba was this elegantly streamlined Douglas Baltimore bomber.

The airstrip is subjected to a very low-level beat-up by an Avro Anson.

Norman investigates the cockpit of a captured Macchi C202 *Folgore* of 96 Squadriglia. Noteworthy items include the sideways-hinging canopy, access flap for the port machine gun, and the distinctive camouflage. A *fasces* emblem can be seen on the engine cowling; a souvenir hunter has cut off the insignia from the tail fin.

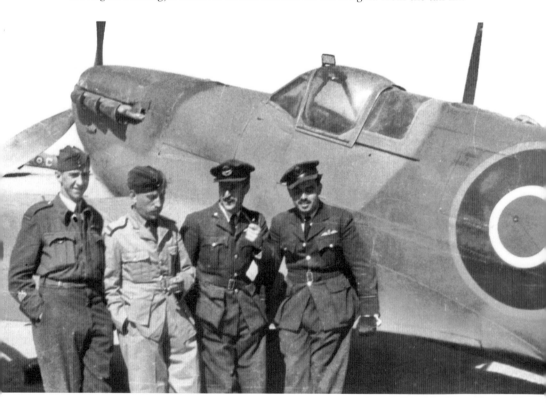

Norman spent some time on ferrying duties after his service with 260 Squadron. Here, third from left, he chats with fellow pilots while leaning on the port wing of a Spitfire V.

*Right:* Another pose, this time in front of a Hurricane IIC, which is apparently named *Slivovica*, after a potent Balkan plum brandy. Note that the fighter's inboard cannon has been removed to reduce the weight.

*Below:* Norman as a flight lieutenant, in front of Spitfire V HB-M – the code letters of 229 Squadron, which served in Malta throughout 1942–43.

Killed on 17 May 1944 in an
accident while CO of 1435
Squadron at Brindisi, Norman
was buried with full military
honours. Here the coffin is
borne into the church while a
military guard presents rifles.

The flag-draped coffin, bearing
his service cap, is carried to the
grave by fellow officers of the
squadron.

Officers and men stand to attention and a final volley is fired before the wreath-covered coffin is laid to rest.

Originally a simple cross was placed over the grave. Norman's remains were later relocated to the Commonwealth War Grave Cemetery in Bari, Southern Italy.

# Flying Officer
# Alan Glover

Alan Glover was born in Chesterfield on 31 December 1922, the only son of a local miner. He joined the VR at the age of eighteen, received his training at 7 ITW Newquay and 6 EFTS Sywell, completed his training at Swift Current, Saskatchawen, and the final refinements were added at 7 OTU Hawarden, back in England. Glover joined 19 Squadron in October 1942 as a sergeant pilot, but in January 1943 his Spitfire was badly shot up by Focke-Wulf 190s on a reconnaissance to Lorient and St Nazaire. He was lucky to return with severe shrapnel wounds to his leg. The last of the fragments were removed as late as 1972. But Alan was flying again eleven weeks later, and after commissioning, and a spell instructing at Burnaston, he joined 3 Squadron in January 1945, flying Hawker Tempests for the rest of the war. He was released in August 1946 and returned to his pre-war job at Staveley Works.

*Above left:* Alan Glover after commissioning in 1944.

*Above right:* Alan photographed in his Spitfire IX while serving with 19 Squadron.

Alan finished his war service flying Hawker Tempests with 3 Squadron. He is pictured with his mount, JF-P, at Volkel, Holland, in early 1945. Other Tempests form an appropriate background.

# Sergeant Pilot
# Richard Thomas Glover

Richard Glover, born at Brailsford in 1918, had a sadly short wartime career. He joined the Derby VR and undertook the elementary flying course with 11 E&RFTS at Prestwick in March–April 1939. After training he was posted from 3 OTU South Cerney to 607 Squadron AAF, but on a familiarisation flight in his Hurricane on 22 June 1940 he was killed when his fighter crashed near Sedgefield, County Durham. The fact that he had only recently joined the unit meant that his accident was never recorded in the Squadron ORB. Richard lies buried in the cemetery at Thornaby-on-Tees, having never met the enemy in combat.

A group image shows Richard on 1 September 1939 at the call-up of Derby RAFVR reservists.

Glover did his advanced tutoring at No. 3 FTS South Cerney. He is shown here top right. Centre front is Sergeant Bill Rolls, later a noted ace. On Rolls' left is Ted Hives, a fellow Derbeian.

# Pilot Officer
# Peter Haldenby

'Pip' Haldenby was born in Derby in 1921, the younger son of the general works manager of the Aero Division at Rolls-Royce Ltd. He was serving as an engineering apprentice at his father's firm when he joined the Derby RAFVR. He gained his 'wings' at 5 FTS Sealand, was commissioned in September 1940, and volunteered for service abroad. He was posted to North Africa and assigned to 73 Squadron in the Western Desert. Described by a colleague as an 'archetypal fighter pilot', Pip was soon heavily involved in the desert war. The Squadron ORB of this time criticised the number of hours flown by the pilots and the effect it was having on the unit as a whole. In February 1941, 73 flew to Tobruk to reinforce 3 Squadron RAAF in defence of the port, which was then under siege from the Afrika Korps. By mid-April, operating inferior Hurricanes against the Luftwaffe, the pilots were low on morale after heavy losses. On 23 April, eight Hurricanes took off to intercept an incoming raid, and while coming in to land after the combat, Pip was attacked from astern, and crashed in flames on the airfield. The Squadron ORB recorded, 'This is a great loss to the squadron of a very fine young lad and a most promising pilot.' He was buried that afternoon in the Tobruk War Cemetery, where he lies alongside other Commonwealth warriors who sacrificed their lives in defence of the vital port.

*Right:* 'Pip' Haldenby in a studio portrait taken before the award of his flying badge.

*Below:* Pip, on the extreme left, is pictured with fellow pilots of 73 Squadron (plus a battered-looking Hurricane 1) at Gazala, Egypt, in March 1941. He was killed on 24 April flying in defence of Tobruk.

# Flight Sergeant Leslie Hemingway

Leslie Hemingway, born at Alvaston on 31 October 1919, was another local fighter pilot never destined to leave his mark on the enemy. The son of a shopkeeper, he became an engineering apprentice with the LMS Railway, and had an early obsession with speed, which may explain his decision to join the Derby VR in October 1938. Upon mobilisation, Laurie was posted to 4 ITW, Bexhill-on-Sea, where he spent the severe winter of 1939–40 before a move in April 1940 to 4 EFTS at Brough, followed by more advanced tutoring at 9 FTS Ansty in early June. He was not impressed with the organisation at the latter, and gladly left for 5 SFTS at Sealand in early July. On 6 September he was awarded his flying badge, and on 19 October he transferred to 7 OTU Hawarden, to complete the final phase of his tutoring. From there he had a short posting to 234 Squadron before moving to the CFS at Upavon in mid-January as an instructor, a move he found somewhat demoralising. This was short-lived however, and in late February he was posted away to 55 OTU at Aston Down, only to find himself back at Hawarden a mere fortnight later. Here he was able to build up his flying hours on Spitfires, doubtless wondering if he would ever graduate to operations. In early May, he was moved to 72 Squadron, and flew dreary patrols off the Northumberland coast before a late June transfer to 611 Squadron, AAF, part of the Hornchurch Wing. He operated the latest Spitfire Vs in aggressive sweeps and Circus missions over Occupied France. Leslie was promoted flight sergeant on 1 July, and soon found that his new unit were suffering from a surfeit of tiring actions. His first mission was uneventful, but the second, on 8 July, was a top cover operation to Circus 41. The high cover were hit by aggressive Me 109s and Hemingway's fighter came under attack. He was apparently seen to bale out safely, but must have come down in the sea. His body was never recovered and his only memorial is his name at Runnymede. Statistically, Leslie was just one more victim of Fighter Command's policy of contesting the airspace over northern France with the Luftwaffe, a policy that left the Germans holding all the tactical advantages.

Leslie Hemingway stands third from left on the back row of this group of Derby reservists in Highfield on 1 September 1939.

# Squadron Leader Lawrence Frederick Henstock

Lawrie Henstock was born in Ashbourne in 1913, the son of the editor of the *Ashbourne Telegraph*. He wished to serve in the RAF but his father persuaded him to join the family printing business. He endured the unendurable for three years before joining an aircraft firm and gaining his flying licence via its subsidised tutoring rates. He then approached the RAF and began pilot training in early 1936 at 7 FTS Peterborough, passing out successfully in October with a posting as pilot officer to 1 Squadron at Tangmere, where he flew Hawker Furies. He then moved to 72 Squadron, initially reformed at Tangmere, but moved to Church Fenton in June. 72 was the first unit to be equipped with the new Gloster Gladiators, the last of the RAFs biplane fighters. He amassed over 400 flying hours on the type before they were replaced by Spitfires in April 1939. By the outbreak of war Lawrie was in command of 'B' Flight, and in December he led them into action against seven Heinkel 111s intercepted north of Arbroath, claiming a share in the two hostiles that were shot down. In February 1940, he was posted to lead 'B' Flight, 64 Squadron, which swapped its lumbering Blenheim 1 'fighters' for Spitfires in April. By May, the squadron was at Kenley, and it took part in operations over Dunkirk, where Lawrie damaged a Me 110. For much of the early part of the summer, 64 Squadron polished up its flying skills. No real action took place until the end of July and early August, when, in a series of actions, he claimed half-shares in a Me 109E and a Dornier 17Z and a probable Me 109. He damaged a Junkers 87 and another Dornier. He had to crash-land his Spitfire on one occasion when the main supercharger bearing on his Merlin engine failed. In early September, Lawrie was posted to the CGS at RAF Warmwell, from where he once took off to repel an enemy raid in a Defiant turret fighter. He and his gunner were lucky to survive when a blazing Me 110 fell out of a cloud and almost hit them. Lawrie remained with the CGS until February 1942, when he was promoted and spent the rest of the war in a series of sedentary posts, including 10 Air Gunners' School, Barrow,

58 OTU at Grangemouth, a series of flying instructors' courses, and a spell at 5 AFU at Tern Hill. After the war, he stayed in the service until 1947, his final post being OC Administration at Hucknall. He tried various jobs before Rolls-Royce took him on in their Technical Publications Department at Derby. He and his wife spent their later years running an antique shop in his native Ashbourne, where he died in March 1981.

Lawrie Henstock as a flight lieutenant early in the Second World War.

Lawrie kitted up for a training flight in Tiger Moth G-ADPE, complete with ring sight, at Witney in 1935.

Lawrie in front of sleek and graceful Hawker Fury K5669 of No. 7 FTS Peterborough in 1936.

Pilot Officer Henstock and his groundcrew pose in front of his usual mount, Gladiator K6141, at Church Fenton, 72 Squadron's base, in 1938. 72 was the last home-based unit to deploy the Gloster biplane.

72 put up this superb formation of Spitfires in line-astern vics during the air display inaugurating Derby's Burnaston Airport in June 1939. Lawrie is leading the last trio, while number two in the leading vic is Flying Officer J. B. Nicolson, later famous as Fighter Command's only Second World War VC.

# Sergeant Pilot
# William Burley Higgins

Burley Higgins was born in September 1913 at Belph, Hodthorpe, near Whitwell. A keen and successful sportsman, he trained as a teacher at Culham College, Abingdon. Described by his tutor as 'a fine, athletic Englishman; open-air type, kindly and good-natured', he taught at his old school until the outbreak of war. He joined the RAFVR in 1937, and learned to fly at 27 E&RFTS Tollerton, near Nottingham. He did his recruit training at 4 ITW Bexhill-on-Sea and progressed to 5 FTS at Sealand in December 1939. He passed out in June 1940 with an 'above average' rating as a pilot and was posted to 32 Squadron at Biggin Hill. While serving with this unit during the summer of 1940, Burley destroyed two Me 109Es and an Me 110, and shared a Dornier 17Z with two other pilots. 32 Squadron was rested at the end of August, but after a spell of leave, he volunteered for further operational flying and joined 253 Squadron, based at Kenley. This unit had suffered heavy casualties during the battle, and Burley was needed to help replace its considerable losses. Once in action, he destroyed an Me 109E and damaged an Me 110, but on 14 September he was shot down and killed at Bredgar, Kent. A local man pulled him from the cockpit of his crashed Hurricane, and wrote to Burley's fiancée, describing his last air action. He was buried at St Lawrence's Church, Whitwell, in a funeral service that attracted most of the local population. Twenty-two years later, his brother Edward Michael, killed when his Derby Airways Dakota crashed in the Pyrenees, was buried in the same plot.

*Right:* Burley Higgins as a sergeant under training at No. 5 SFTS Sealand in December 1939.

*Below:* Burley completed a two-year teacher-training course at Culham College, Abingdon, where he excelled in sporting activities. He is standing second from left in this shot of the college cricket XI.

An austere and scholarly academic occupies the centre of the 1935/36 football team shot. Burley is seated on the extreme right.

'D' Flight, 45 Course, 5 SFTS Sealand in spring 1940 – the first intake to train on the Miles Master 1. Burley stands in the middle row, second from left, with Ray Holmes on his left and 'Wag' Haw third left in the top row. Holmes helped shoot down the Dornier 17 that fell on Victoria Station on 15 September 1940, while Haw was a rare British recipient of the Order of Lenin for service in Russia in 1941.

Celebrations are in progress as 45 Course complete their training at Sealand in the late spring of 1940. Burley can be seen just above the left shoulder of the balding, moustached officer boasting medal ribbons, obviously a senior figure at the station.

The bullet-riddled Dornier 17Z of 8/KG77 (3Z+GS) shot down by Higgins' Blue Section, 32 Squadron, on 3 July 1940, lies at rest in a Kentish hopfield at Baybrooks, Horsmonden.

Lady spectators look on with interest from the left as an airman inspects the spread-eagle insignia of KG77 under the cockpit of the wrecked Dornier.

Burley's last victory was an Me 109E piloted by Hauptmann Ernst Wiggers of JG 51, whose funeral pyre can be seen blazing in a field near Lewes, Sussex, on 11 September 1940. Lorries have halted on the nearby A27 Brighton Road to view the remains of the burning fighter.

# Flight Lieutenant Frederick Meakin

Fred 'Masher' Meakin was born in Derby on 21 March 1921, the son of a local grocer. After studying at Derby Technical College he joined LMS Railway as a clerk. He volunteered for the RAFVR in February 1941 and following basic instruction, was sent to Canada in September as part of the Empire Air Training scheme. He received his flying tuition at 13 Elementary and 13 SFTS schools, gaining his 'wings' and a commission in the process. Fred returned home in May 1942 for the final refinements, which were supplied by 7 AFDU and 57 OTU Hawarden. In October, he progressed to 167 Squadron at Ludham in Norfolk, where he flew Spitfire Vs on low-level missions. On one occasion he was lucky to walk away when he force-landed after hitting telephone wires on a practice flight. In February 1943 the squadron added escort missions to its schedule, but in March Fred was sent overseas to Australia, where he eventually joined 54 Squadron at Darwin. 54 had been an element in 1 Fighter Wing, sent out in 1942 to defend Northern Australia from Japanese air attacks flying from New Guinea. However, by the time Fred had become part of the unit in November 1943, the threat had receded. Spitfire VIIIs replaced the ageing Mk Vs in April 1944 and on 2 July Fred and a fellow pilot intercepted and shot down a Japanese reconnaissance aeroplane, a fast and high-flying Mitsubishi Ki 46 Dinah. It remains the only Japanese warplane shot down by a Derbyshire pilot. Three days later, Fred was killed when his aircraft clipped a tree while circling after take-off from Drysdale Airfield. He was buried in the Adelaide River War Cemetery, Northern Territory, with full military honours, leaving his Australian fiancée to mourn her loss.

The only Japanese aircraft shot down by a Derbyshire pilot was a Mitsubishi Ki 46
Dinah reconnaissance machine, shared between Fred 'Masher' Meakin and a fellow
pilot of 54 Squadron over the Timor Sea, Australia, on 20 July 1944.

# Pilot Officer
# Frank Mellor DFM

Frank Mellor was born on 30 September 1921 at Whaley Bridge, the son of a quarry owner and haulier. He studied at Buxton College before working for his grandfather in the quarry industry. He volunteered for the RAF in February 1941 and did his initial training at 4 ITW Paignton before leaving for Canada in August. Frank's service continued at 31 SFTS Calgary and 34 SFTS Medicine Hat, Alberta. He gained his flying badge in February 1942, was promoted to sergeant pilot, and returned to complete his instruction in England. Frank had long expressed a desire to fly multi-engined bombers, but was drafted onto single-seat fighters for his pains. After a spell with 7 PRC Harrogate and 5 AFU, he moved to 55 OTU at Aston Down, where he received an 'above average' assessment for his flying. He and a friend also indulged in a low-level 'beat up' of his native Buxton in their Spitfires on 12 August, thrilling the local populace, and that same month Frank was posted to 165 Squadron. The posting was short-lived, and in September he was reassigned to 111 Squadron, which headed for North Africa via Gibraltar at the end of November. The unit's Spitfire Vs were assembled there and 111 flew off to its Algerian airfield. Conditions were poor, with rain and muddy airstrips. The squadron operated without initial radar cover, which necessitated the maintenance of standing patrols. Between February and May 1943, Frank destroyed an Me 109F and shared in no less than three other 'kills' – two more 109s and a Focke-Wulf 190. He also claimed a probable Me 110 and damaged two other 109Fs, one of which was almost certainly shot down. In early May, Frank was commissioned, and in June, 111 flew to Safi, Malta, where they were re-equipped with Spitfire IXs in preparation for the attack on Sicily. On 24 June, Frank added a rare Me 410 twin-motor reconnaissance fighter to his tally, but on 3 July his engine was hit in combat while 111 was covering an attack on Biscari Airfield, Sicily. He was escorted part of the way back to Malta by Wing Commander 'Cocky' Dundas, but with the island in sight, Dundas left him to assist another pilot, and Frank failed to return. His body was later recovered off the Sicilian coast, and he was buried at Catania War Cemetery. The Squadron ORB referred to him as 'one of our most valuable pilots'. Almost a year later, he was awarded a DFM, gazetted for the day before his death. Frank's family remain proud of him and his achievements, and his medal is in the safe-keeping of his nephew.

Frank Mellor, taken in a Tiger Moth while a pilot undergoing training in Canada with 31 EFTS Calgary in late 1941.

Frank appears to be digging himself into a deep hole in this shot. While his rank is LAC, his white forage cap flash indicates his status as an officer cadet. However, he did not gain a commission until shortly before his death in 1943.

Frank and friend are obviously roughing it as they shave by the side of a lake, again perhaps in Canada.

Frank became the first trainee in his course to solo in Canada, and received his 'wings' shortly after. Here, in this snowy scene, he is in company with an AC1 friend, who wears a wireless operator's badge.

On leave in his native Buxton, Frank takes a stroll in a local park. On one occasion, he and a fellow pilot shook up the spa in August 1942 with a low-level beat up in their Spitfires.

Frank is standing fifth from the right on the back row in this line-up of officer and NCO pilots in front of a Spitfire V – probably at 55 OTU, Aston Down, in mid-1942.

In this official picture, Frank is shown bartering for eggs with a Tunisian Arab in the spring of 1943. The distant Spitfires of 111 Squadron form an appropriate backdrop to the scene.

Several of Frank's victims in North Africa were Messerschmitt 109Gs, similar to this example preserved at Duxford Air Museum in Cambridgeshire.

The Messerschmitt 410 twin-motor fighter was a *rara avis*, although Frank shot one down off Cape Passaro in Sicily, on 24 June 1943 – his final combat victory.

# Flight Lieutenant Michael John Sharpe Mycroft DFC, Belgian CdG

Mike Mycroft was born in Clay Cross on 14 October 1920, the son of a timber merchant, and he worked in the family business until June 1940, when he enlisted in the RAF and was sent to the United States for training in June 1941. The Southern Aviation School, Camden, USAAC, pronounced him 'washed out' for 'lack of progress' in July of that year. 'Couldn't care less' was the rejoinder in Mike's logbook, as in August he moved to 3 BFTS at Miami, Oklahoma, where he completed his tutelage and was commissioned in January 1942. Back in England he progressed to 17 AFU at Watton in May, followed by 56 OTU at Sutton Bridge in June, from where he was posted to 32 (Hurricane) Squadron at West Malling in September. In November, 32 relocated to North Africa, and Mike remained with the unit in Algeria until the following autumn. In early 1944 he joined 1 TEU at Kinnel, where his flying was rated as 'above average', and in June he moved to 349 (Belgian) Squadron, part of 135 Wing, 84 Group, 2nd TAF, flying Spitfires. From this date until the end of the war he was occupied mainly in escorts, sweeps and ground-attack missions with cannon and bombs, often carried out in the face of heavy enemy flak. One memorable operation was on the German HQ at Oostburg in Belgium during the assault on the town in October 1944. Mike was awarded a DFC and a Belgian CdG for his service, the former citation recording that he had destroyed or damaged over forty-five locomotives and barges and over forty-five transport vehicles. 'This officer,' it concluded, 'has at all times shown enthusiasm in his attacks, together with outstanding courage and determination.' Mike left the RAF in 1946 and returned to the family business, finding time to indulge in his interests in classical music, golf, tennis and swimming. He died in 1960, shortly after his sixtieth birthday.

*Left:* Mike Mycroft after commissioning in early 1942. Although a fighter pilot, Mike spent most of his service flying ground-attack missions.

*Below:* Mike did his initial flying training in America. In this evocative shot, he pilots a North American Harvard trainer at the Miami, Oklahoma FTS in August 1941.

With the Volunteer Reserve badges on his collar, Mike chats to his father, a timber merchant in his native Clay Cross.

Mike, on the left, wearing his Mae West, takes time off for a drink while serving as a flight commander with 349 (Belgian) Squadron, part of 135 Wing, 84 Group, 2nd TAF in France, in the summer of 1944.

Mike, on the right, checks in with his squadron commander, Van der Velde. The strain of constant close-support missions clearly shows on his face.

A fine air-to-air shot, showing Mike piloting his Spitfire LFIX (GZ-V) over France. As well as the award of the DFC, Mike received the Belgian Croix de Guerre for his services with 349.

# Sergeant Pilot
# Henry Press-Dee Morgan

Harry Press-Dee Morgan, born in 1922 in Derby, was the half-brother of Alan Feary. He joined the RAFVR in late 1941 and after gaining his 'wings' served in a training capacity before joining 41 Squadron at Merston in July 1941. Harry's Spitfire was shot down on 27 August when 41 was the Tactical Support Wing to Circus 85. His body was retrieved from the English Channel and buried in Hawkinge Cemetery.

Harry Press-Dee Morgan trained as a fighter pilot and was killed in action in Spitfire 11b R7223 on 27 August 1941.

# Warrant Officer
# Alan Percival Pugh

Alan Pugh was born in Derby on 30 May 1921, the son of a carpenter. Pre-war, he was working as a clerk when he volunteered for the RAF. He was sent to the USA for pilot training in September 1941, returned in the spring of 1942, and completed his instruction at 2 FIS Dalcross and 17 AFS Watton. He was then trapped in a ten-month spell at 1 Signals Station, Cranwell, mainly flying WT exercises. He was finally posted to 55 OTU, Llandow, and latterly 53 OTU Kirton-in-Lindsey, from whence he progressed to 64 (Spitfire) Squadron – stationed at Ayr as a sergeant pilot. By the time he reached his new unit, he had amassed nearly 1,000 hours' flying experience. His sixteen-month spell with 64 was spent mostly on escorts, sweeps and strafing attacks on land targets and enemy ships, plus support missions on D-Day on 6 June 1944. The squadron's Spitfire Vs were replaced with IXs shortly after the invasion, and 64 continued its low-level strafing, interspersed with sweeps and bomber escorts. In September, Alan helped protect Dakotas supply dropping over Arnhem, before his promotion to warrant officer and a posting to Australia, where, after a refresher course at 8 OTU Parkes in early 1945, he joined 54 Squadron at Darwin. He did little flying in this backwater, and returned to England in the autumn, joining 12 Group Command, Hucknall, before a move to 263 Squadron at Church Fenton. He served with 263 for two years, flying various marks of the Gloster Meteor, and in 1949 joined 1 OFU, delivering a variety of aeroplanes all over the world. He left the service that October, but rejoined in April 1951 as a Pilot 1. After short spells at 101 FRS Finningley and CFS South Cerney, he was back with the OFU in October. Two months later, this unit were tasked with delivering Canadair-built North American Sabre F86E jet fighters across the Atlantic to Britain. The Sabres staged from Canada through Greenland and Iceland before landing at Prestwick, Ayr. On 19 December, Alan was on the final stage from Keflavik in XB534 – one of the first jets to be flown to the UK – when he apparently ran out of fuel on 'finals' into Prestwick. There was a suggestion that he swung his fighter away from a built-up area and crashed in a nearby field, leaving no time to eject. Alan was buried, with full military honours, in a grave alongside the airfield where his lone flight should have ended. This fine pilot died while pursuing an essential task.

A post-war image of Alan Pugh, taken while he was serving with 263 Squadron.

Warrant Officer Pugh sits centre front in this group of flyers of 64 Squadron, in 1944.

Alan was killed while ferrying North American Sabre F86E (XB534) – identical to the machines seen here – from Canada to Britain in December 1952. The fighter crashed in Ayrshire en route to Prestwick.

# Pilot Officer
# Nathaniel William Rowell

Nat Rowell was born in Matlock. After training he was posted to 131 Squadron, operating from Merston. On 5 June 1942 he was shot down in combat with JG 2 off Le Havre while operating as part of the Escort Wing to Circus 188. He is commemorated on the Runnymede Memorial.

Nat Rowell is shown in the cockpit of Presentation Spitfire Vb BL327 *Rochester* while serving with 131 Squadron. He was shot down in Spitfire Vb BL250 (NX-S) on 5 June 1942 off Le Havre in combat with fighters of JG 2.

# Air Commodore
# Philip James Sanders DFC

Philip Sanders was born in Chesterfield on 1 May 1911, the son of a local solicitor. After an education at Cheltenham and Balliol College, Oxford, he commenced articles in the City, but realising he was not cut out for the law, he joined the RAF on a Permanent Commission in March 1936. He trained at 5 FTS Sealand, emerging with a 'Distinguished Pass', and was posted to 1 Squadron at Tangmere. He remained with the unit until August 1939, when he was appointed Sector Operations Officer and Fighter Controller at Hornchurch. In late May 1940, he became CO of 92 Squadron, flying Spitfires, and in operations over Dunkirk in early June he shot down a Heinkel 111 and claimed a second probable. After a spell at Pembrey in South Wales, the squadron was moved to Biggin Hill in early September, where it took part in the latter stages of the Battle of Britain. In just fifteen days of fighting, Philip destroyed two Heinkel 111s, two Me 109Es and a Dornier 17Z, together with two more 109 probables. On 23 September, he donned a uniform jacket carrying an oil stain that his batman had cleaned with 100-octane petrol. Philip lit a cigarette and the ensuing flames inflicted minor burns to his hands, which led to a month's rest from operations. He was awarded a DFC and following recuperation was moved to HQ 11 Group, where he concentrated on night operations. In June 1941 he became CO of 264 Squadron, flying Defiants and the ill-starred 'Turbinlite' Havocs, fitted with nose-mounted searchlights. Promoted wing commander, Sanders went to the USA as fighter test pilot at the US Experimental Station at Wright Field, Ohio, where he flew the first American jet fighter, the Bell Airacomet. Back in England, he joined the HQ staff of 84 Group, 2nd TAF, and in February 1945 he was group captain commanding an OTU at Petan Tiqua in Palestine. He reverted to wing commander rank in October 1946, and served at the Air Ministry before becoming air attaché in Belgrade in 1948–51. After a spell as Wing Commander Flying at Coltishall, he was promoted group captain in charge of RAF Leeming, followed by a posting to SHAPE in Paris, and a memorable tour as air attaché in Moscow in 1958–61 at the height of the Kruschev era. Sanders achieved air rank in 1961 and his final posting was as Air Commodore Operations at HQ Fighter Command. On retirement in 1962 he served fourteen years at the MOD as a civil servant. Philip retired to Sussex, where he died on 22 January 1989.

A charcoal portrait of Squadron Leader Sanders DFC, drawn by Sir William Rothenstein in November 1940.

A photograph of Philip taken late in the war, after his operational service had finished.

Air Commodore Sanders and Wing Commander Billy Drake pictured at a No. 1 Squadron reunion in 1962, twenty-four years after their service together with the unit.

# Pilot Officer
# Douglas Clayton Shepley

Douglas Shepley was born in Carlton-in-Lindrick in 1918, but from the age
of eight he lived at Woodthorpe Hall at Holmesfield in North Derbyshire. He
was educated at Oundle School, and after a short time in the family business
followed his elder brother Rex into the RAF. He attended the RAF College,
Cranwell, and graduated in September 1939, when he joined 152 Squadron
at Acklington. Both his sister Jeanne and his brother Rex were killed in the
early part of the war, the former drowned when her ship the SS *Yorkshire*
was torpedoed off Gibraltar by U37, the latter shot down in his Lysander in a
supply mission over Dunkirk. 152 was moved to Warmwell in July 1940, and in
operations off the south coast, Douglas claimed two Me 109Es destroyed and
a Junkers 88 damaged. On 12 August his Spitfire was lost over the Channel,
and Douglas became the third of the Shepley siblings to die in under a year. His
mother and young widow raised the money, mainly in the locality, to purchase
a Presentation Spitfire Vb (W3649), which carried the family name. The
warplane was subsequently the mount of Group Captain F. V. Beamish, leader
of the Kenley Wing. Beamish claimed three enemy warplanes flying *Shepley*,
plus a share in a fourth, but was lost with the aircraft over the Channel on
28 March 1942. In 1979, a public house in Totley, Sheffield, close by
Woodthorpe Hall, and named the Shepley Spitfire, was opened by Douglas's
only surviving brother, Seymour. The inn sign carries an image of Douglas
himself.

*Left:* Pilot Officer
Shepley in a studio
portrait taken after
commissioning in
October 1939.

*Below:* Douglas in the
cockpit of his Hawker
Audax trainer K4384
while training at
Cranwell RAF College
in 1939. Note the four
20 lb Cooper practice
bombs under the port
wing.

Spitfire 1 (UM-H) undergoing a thorough service check at Acklington, where Douglas served with 152 Squadron. Note the tractor-towed petrol bowser on the right.

Douglas's Spitfire K9999 (UM-S), with UM-R alongside, in a snowy scene during the bitter Northumberland winter of 1940. Parachutes can be seen on the port wingtips, and both fighters have their starter trolleys plugged in.

*Left:* Douglas clad in flying gear in Acklington in early 1940.

*Below:* Douglas relaxes at Acklington in the early summer of 1940, with Spitfires of the unit, including UM-M, in the near distance.

The cockpit of *Shepley*, the family's Presentation Spitfire, shows clear details of the armoured windscreen, reflector gunsight, and rear-view mirror.

*Above left:* The war memorial in Holmesfield churchyard reveals the extensive sacrifices of the Shepley family, who lost three of their children to Hitler's soaring ambition.

*Above right:* In 1979, a newly built local public house was given the name the Shepley Spitfire. In its latest incarnation, the inn sign shows both the aircraft and Douglas Shepley himself.

# Flight Lieutenant
# Norman Taylor DFC DFM AE

Norman Taylor was born at Chellaston on 23 October 1920, and trained as an apprentice at the Standard Motor Company at Coventry with the ambition of becoming a test pilot. He joined the RAFVR and was granted leave from his work to undertake the two-month course in initial flying training at 11 E&RFTS Ayr in April–May 1939. When war broke out, he went to 3 ITW at St Leonards-on-Sea, resuming his apprenticeship in early 1940 while awaiting a further posting, but able to brush up on his airmanship at 9 E&RFTS Ansty. In March 1940, he reported to 10 SFTS at Tern Hill, and in June he was lucky to pull off a forced landing when the throttle of his Harvard trainer jammed. His aeroplane caught fire as he scrambled clear. He was graded as 'above average' and moved on to 6 OTU Sutton Bridge in July before a posting to 601 Squadron AAF at Tangmere in early August, just in time to take part in the Battle of Britain. In just over two months of intensive fighting, Norman shot down a Junkers 87, an Me 109E and a Dornier 17Z, and shared in the destruction of a Junkers 88 and a Heinkel 111. He also claimed a Junkers 88 probable and damaged an Me 110. When he destroyed the 109, his Hurricane was hit by the German fighter's wingman and he had to bale out over Gravesend. In late September, the battle-weary unit were rested and moved to Exeter. They moved again to Northolt in early 1941, operating Hurricane 11Bs, and after a short spell with 1 ADU at Hendon in April, Taylor returned to claim an Me 110, an Me 109E and two 109Fs destroyed, plus a 109 damaged, in May–June. During the latter month, he was awarded a DFM and was commissioned. He then volunteered for the Merchant Ship Fighter Unit (MSFU), flying catapult-launched 'Hurricats' off 'CAM ships' (Catapult Armed Merchant Ships). He was tasked with shooting down long-range enemy reconnaissance aircraft far out in the Atlantic Ocean. Norman completed voyages to Canada and Gibraltar, and on 1 November 1942 he was launched from *Empire Gale* and shot down a Focke-Wulf 200C Condor off the coast of Spain, a feat that led to the award of an immediate

DFC. In baling out from his Hurricane after the action, he almost drowned before being rescued. Norman remained with the MSFU until April 1943, earning an 'above average' assessment for his flying skills. He was posted to Rolls-Royce in Derby as an instructor and gained an Air Efficiency medal; he remained there until the end of 1945. He then progressed to 245 Meteor Squadron at Colerne, and later to 222, another Meteor unit, where he commanded 'B' Flight and participated in victory flypasts over the Channel Islands and London during the summer. In July 1947 he was part of the RAF escort to the battleship HMS *Vanguard* – which was taking the Royal Family on an official visit to South Africa – and then he moved to 33 Squadron, which flew Tempest 11s from Fassberg in Germany. In October 1947 he completed an instructor's course at the Empire Flying School, and his final move was to the Station Flight, 135 Wing, RAF Gutersloh, in early 1948. On 29 April the Harvard trainer he was flying lost power on approach to the airfield and crashed, killing Norman and his passenger. He was buried at Gütersloh, at the age of twenty-seven.

A studio portrait of Pilot Officer Norman Taylor DFM, taken shortly after he gained his commission in the summer of 1941.

*Above left:* Norman at No. 11 E&RFTS, Prestwick, in March 1939. He is about to fly his first solo in Tiger Moth L6949 (G-AFFA).

*Above right:* Tomfoolery on the course, with Norman second from right. The name of the airman presenting his posterior remains unknown.

An Avro Tutor, one of the elementary trainers in use at Prestwick.

A Fairey Battle light bomber at Prestwick. These aeroplanes were already obsolescent by the start of the war, and were massacred by the Luftwaffe during the Battle of France. A row of Ansons can be seen in the near distance.

This lumbering Handley Page Heyford night bomber was also on view at Prestwick. Fortunately these antediluvian relics had been phased out of service by the time war began.

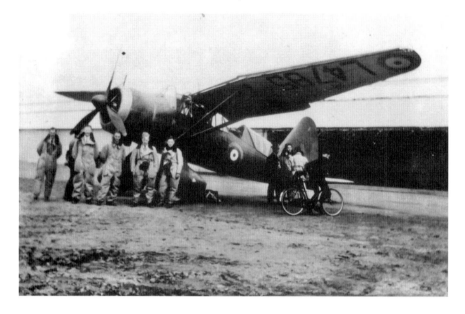

*Above:* Norman is at the centre of the group in flying kit. The Westland Lysander L4785 army co-operation aircraft was visiting Prestwick at the time.

*Left:* Sergeant Taylor on the left, apparently boasting a transient moustache, strolls along the front at Hastings in December 1939, accompanied by Sergeant Woolley. Both airmen carry compulsory gas masks. At the time Norman was with 3 ITW on the south coast.

Norman, fifth from left, joins the line-up of 601 Squadron pilots sometime during the Battle of Britain.

On 31 August, Norman shot down an Me 109E, although he was himself shot down by the German's No. 2 and had to bale out. The 109, from JG 77, crash-landed near Gravesend with the pilot badly burned. Firemen, soldiers and civilians inspect the partly burned-out wreckage.

*Left:* Sergeant pilots on readiness pose by a 601 Hurricane during the autumn of 1940. Norman is the tall figure at the rear; the other three, from right to left, are sergeants Jensen, Hetherington and Weightman.

*Below:* Norman joined the MSFU in 1941 and his first trip was to Halifax, Nova Scotia, in November 1941 and on board the *Empire Rowan*. The two-way voyage was hazardous, with heavy gales in both directions. Here, Hurricane V7253 is pounded by strong seas on its way back to England in January 1942.

In May 1942, Taylor joined *Empire Gale* on the Gibraltar run. In this shot, Norman sits on the cowling of Hurricane V6927 on the outward passage.

Norman and fellow pilot Joe Birbeck perch on Hurricat V6927, which is mounted on the merchantman's fo'c'sle catapult. The LU code indicates a pool-unit aircraft earmarked for the MSFU.

A studio shot of Norman, probably taken during his spell in Gibraltar in June–October 1942.

On the Gibraltar run, Norman's fellow pilot was Joe Birbeck, seen on the left. Here the pair enjoy the sunshine in a convenient part of the deck.

Norman (left) and Joe, Mae Wests donned for action, pose by the *Empire Gale*'s rail on the way to the Mediterranean.

Norman was in Gibraltar during the period of the Malta convoys, when it was vital to resupply the island base. He took this (probably illicit) shot of the elderly battleship HMS *Malaya*, which was part of the Operation Harpoon escort (11–16 June 1942). The 16-inch gun turrets of the leviathan can be clearly seen, as can the stern of the carrier HMS *Eagle* on the left.

HMS *Eagle* approaches Gibraltar in the run-up to *Harpoon*, its Sea Hurricanes of 801 Squadron visible on the flight deck. Sadly, the hard-worked old vessel was sunk on 11 August by U73 while covering Operation *Pedestal*, another Malta convoy.

In late October 1942, Norman embarked on CAM ship *Empire Heath* for the return voyage to England. Here, Hurricat V7070 is hoisted on its catapult trolley as protection for the home-bound convoy.

A frontal view of Hurricane V7070 clearly shows details of the trolley and the short take-off ramp. The figure on the cockpit is Paddy O'Sullivan, the CAM ship's second pilot.

250 miles west of Spain, V7070 perches on its cradle a few hours before its combat with a KG40 Focke-Wulf 200C Condor. The ramp is offset to prevent smoke and flames from the blast-off damaging the bridge, and to ensure that in the event of a mislaunch the ship does not run down a ditched pilot.

The uninviting pilot's-eye view of the incredibly diminutive catapult ramp
– necessitating a force of 3.5 g at blast-off.

The Luftwaffe's scourge of the Atlantic was the Focke-Wulf 200 Condor, which had
a vast range and could shadow Allied convoys in mid-Atlantic.

After shooting down the Condor, Norman nearly drowned before a boat from the corvette HMS *Sweet Briar* rescued him from the ocean. Here, the weathered old veteran approaches Norman's CAM ship to safely return the successful pilot.

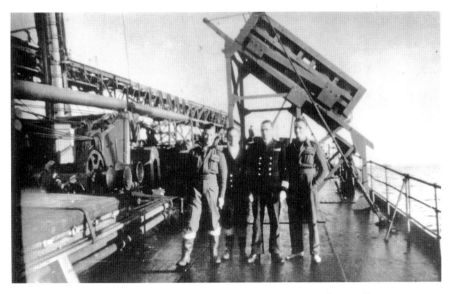

The day following the action, Norman, on the right, poses with O'Sullivan, 'Ginger' Ward, the fighter direction officer, and Captain Hamnett. The launch ramp at the top left is now vacant.

Thirty-seven years on, Norman receives the supreme accolade as the hero on the front page of the 'Victor' comic.

Wearing the ribbons of the DFC (for the Condor episode) and DFM, Flying Officer Taylor relaxes with an archetypal-looking pilot identified only as 'Smithy'.

Norman is here pictured with a Hurricane in the background, an image probably taken at Hucknall Airfield while he was posted with Rolls-Royce in Derby.

By early 1946, Norman was flying Gloster Meteor jets with 222 Squadron as OC 'B' Flight. He stands fifth from right in front of Meteor III MR-N at the Exeter base.

A good study of MR-N, with pilot Jimmy Walker posing for the camera. Note the ports for the left-hand 20 mm cannon to his right.

On 29 April 1948, Norman took off from his Gütersloh base in Harvard IIB KF569. The aircraft lost power and spun in near Wünsdorf, killing him and his passenger. He was buried at Gütersloh, and his tombstone bears the proud inscription 'ONE OF THE FEW'.

# Flight Lieutenant John Edward van Schaick DFM

'Jacky' van Schaick was born in St Helens on 21 June 1921, but the family moved to Littleover, Derby, in 1930, and John's father joined the staff of Air Schools Ltd at Burnaston on its formation in 1938. The family boasted Dutch antecedents, their forebears having emigrated from the Netherlands in 1856, and John was the nephew of William van Schaick of Pilkington Brothers, the internationally famous glass manufacturers. His Uncle Leonard earned the DCM and MM as an RFC observer in the First World War and his father was an NCO instructor in the RFC and RAF in the same conflict. John was employed by the Derbyshire Building Society on leaving school, and he joined the Derby VR on reaching the age of eighteen. When war broke out he went to 3 ITW at St Leonards-on-Sea, progressing to 4 EFTS at Brough for his *ab initio* flying training. He passed on to 9 SFTS at Ansty in mid-June, while a further move to 1 SFTS Netheravon lasted until August, when he received his flying brevet with an 'average' assessment. The final flying polish was provided by 7 OTU at Hawarden, before his posting to 266 Squadron at Wittering in early November 1940, where an intensive training regime fitted him for operational flying. While with 266 he shot down a Junkers 88 off Skegness, and during an early fighter sweep over France he claimed an Me 109F probable and damaged a second. In July he moved on to 609 Squadron AAF at Biggin Hill, and during the summer and autumn he destroyed an Me 109F with another 109 probable and two more damaged. On 1 November he was decorated with the DFM. He was commissioned in early December. In early February 1942 he was posted to 137 Squadron at Matlask as a flight lieutenant and OC 'B' Flight. 137 flew Westland Whirlwind twin-motor fighters, and John served with the unit for most of the year, through the changeover from convoy patrols to fighter-bomber duties. The Whirlwinds carried two 250 lb bombs. The unit was tasked with anti-shipping and land targets, and on 31 October John was hit by flak and forced to ditch in the sea off Boulogne, in the middle of a German minefield. A Walrus amphibian of 77 Squadron pulled off a most gallant rescue, plucking John from the water in an air-sea rescue epic that was widely reported in the media of the day. In early December, he was posted to 59 OTU Milfield, although he was granted leave in mid-January 1943 to marry in Littleover and honeymoon in Torquay. On 20 February 1943 his Miles Master trainer went out of control, crashing at Berrington, near Berwick, killing both occupants. John was buried at St Peter's, Littleover, in an impressive military funeral held at the church he had been married in just over a month earlier. He was yet another fine Derbyshire aviator who perished in a flying accident.

A crayon portrait of John van Schaick taken after commissioning in late 1941.

Looking no more than fifteen years old, John sits cross-legged second from left in the group portrait of the Derby VR taken on 1 September 1939. Above his left shoulder is Sergeant John Anderson, who later trained as a fighter pilot.

John as a sergeant in mid-1940.

A Blackburn B2 side-by-side biplane trainer identical to the one John flew at No. 4 EFTS, Brough, in the early months of 1940.

John served in 609 Squadron, Alan Feary's old unit, in 1941. Here he poses in the cockpit of a Spitfire V of 'B' Flight, one of the squadron's mounts – again looking incredibly youthful.

*Right:* The DFM awarded to van Schaick on 1 November 1941.

*Below:* In early 1942, John was posted to 137 Squadron, which flew Westland Whirlwinds, twin-motor fighters armed with four 20 mm cannon mounted in the nose.

John, on the right, by now a flight lieutenant, chats with a fellow pilot behind the starboard wing of Whirlwind SF-V.

Deckchairs and Lloyd Loom pattern seating abound as 137 pilots relax at their dispersal at Matlaske on a sunny day in 1942. John is visible second from right in Mae West and flying boots. In the near distance, a Whirlwind awaits its pilot.

A 'Whirlibomber' carrying a 250 lb bomb beneath each wings. Note the projecting barrels of the four cannon in the nose, which were capable of delivering a fearsome punch.

John chatting with HM Queen Elizabeth during her visit to an RAF exhibition, south of England, autumn 1942.

The Supermarine Walrus, affectionately known as the 'Shagbat', was a pusher amphibian much used for air-sea rescues during the Second World War.

This posed photograph shows the difficulties in helping downed aircrew into the rescue plane, due to its low fuselage profile when settled on the water. The observer needed brute strength to haul soaked aviators to safety.

*The Rescue* is a dramatic impression of the 277 Squadron Walrus taking off through a German minefield after pulling van Schaick from the sea on 31 October 1942.

A Miles Master Mk I similar to the machine in which John was killed on 20 February 1943.

*Left:* RAF officers bear John's beflagged coffin to its resting place in St Peter's churchyard, Littleover, Derby. His newlywed wife, Marion ('Pat') heads the mourning procession behind.

*Below:* John's headstone in St Peter's churchyard. His father Harry is interred in the same grave.

PER ARDUA AD ASTRA
IN PROUD AND CHERISHED MEMORY OF
JOHN EDWARD VAN SCHAICK. D.F.M.
FLIGHT LIEUTENANT, R.A.F.V.R.
KILLED ON ACTIVE SERVICE
20TH FEBRUARY 1943, AGED 21 YEARS.
ONE OF "THE FEW."
ALSO OF HIS LOVING FATHER
HARRY VAN SCHAICK.
AT REST 26TH JAN 1960, AGED 65 YEARS.
WAITING FOR THE COMING OF OUR LORD JESUS CHRIST.

# Flight Sergeant
# John William Wagstaffe

Bill Wagstaffe was born in Chesterfield in 1919, the son of the head porter
at the Royal Hospital. Educated in Chesterfield, he joined the Birmingham
City Police, but volunteered for the RAFVR in 1941. He was sent to Southern
Rhodesia for training and was posted to 93 Squadron when he returned to
England. On 8 September 1944, his Spitfire IX was shot down by enemy flak
at Bligny-sur-Ouche, France. The local villagers buried him in the churchyard
at Bessey-la-Cour, where he still lies.

Bill is shown preparing for a flight in a Tiger Moth in the African sunshine. Sadly he
was shot down by flak and killed over France in September 1944 while flying Spitfires
with 93 Squadron.

Bill Wagstaffe did his pilot training in Southern Rhodesia. This portrait was taken shortly after he gained his 'wings'.

# Flying Officer
# John Alwyne Wain

Alwyne Wain was born in Darley Dale on 12 April 1921, the son of an engine driver on the LMS Railway. A promising and athletic student, he intended to make a career in the Civil Service, but volunteered for the RAF. While awaiting his call-up, he opted for temporary work in the offices of Glapwell Colliery, and on his first day, with heavy snow and no transport, he walked ten miles with two heavy suitcases in order to not let his employers down. He was called up in April 1940 and completed his basic instruction at 3 ITW St Leonards-on-Sea, progressing to 7 EFTS Desford, 12 FTS Grantham and 54 OTU at Church Fenton. Sergeant Pilot Wain was posted in late May 1941 to 151 Squadron, Wittering, operating obsolescent Defiant 11 turret night fighters. An enthusiastic sportsman and gardener, his keenness, general ability and willingness to help with ATC cadets who visited the base caught the eye of his station commander, Basil Embry, who was responsible for commissioning him in December 1941. While flying Defiants, his gunner claimed damage to two Dornier 217s during night sorties, and in March 1942 he accompanied the destroyer HMS *Verdun* on an east coast convoy escort, presumably to gain some understanding of air-sea liaison and its problems. In April 1942, the squadron re-equipped with the de Havilland Mosquito 11. Piloting this superb aircraft, Alwyne shot down a Heinkel 111 and damaged a Dornier 217. On 10 August, he was vectored onto a German raider, reporting by R/T that he had it in sight fifty miles out to sea. His aircraft never returned, and its wreckage was reported by an ASR launch the following morning, presumably shot down by the bomber they had intercepted. He was another fine young hero England could ill afford to lose, and Alwyne's seniors recorded their appreciation of his professional abilities in several letters to his family. His memorial is Panel 72 at Runnymede; his only grave is the sea.

Pilot Officer Wain, newly commissioned in 1942.

151 Squadron parades in front of a unit Defiant two-seat turret night fighter at Wittering. Alwyn is standing sixth from left. 151 was the last squadron to use these obsolescent fighters operationally.

A fine shot of Alwyne's black-painted Defiant DZ-B, in its blast pen. Alwyn poses on the wing, flanked by fellow aircrew.

Alwyne, in full gear, is shown strapped in the strictly functional cockpit of his Defiant. The four-gun turret behind him provided the only armament carried by this misconceived aeroplane.

151 re-equipped with the formidable De Havilland Mosquito Mk II from April 1942. One of these outstanding aircraft is seen here in flight.

# Pilot Officer
# Francis Richard Walker-Smith

Frank Walker-Smith was born in Spondon on 29 January 1917. He was a
Rolls-Royce apprentice, although from an early age he felt flying was in his
blood and wanted to pursue a career in the RAF. His only other interest was
sport. He was interviewed for a permanent commission, but failed the medical
as he had slight astigmatism, although it hardly seemed a serious problem.
Frank joined the Derby VR, and during training often flew his Tiger Moth
over Spondon, performing unauthorised aerobatics above his parents' home
to the chagrin of his neighbours, who predicted his early demise in some
spectacular accident. He was only the second of the local VRs to gain his
'wings' (Alan Feary being the first) and upon mobilisation he was posted to
9 FTS at Thornaby-on-Tees in December 1939, followed by a move to 5 OTU
Aston Down the following March. In May he joined 85 Squadron, then in
France, although it remains highly doubtful if he saw action in the confused
days before the unit became non-operational through lack of Hurricanes.
He was ordered back to Debden, where he had plenty of time to hone his
operational flying skills as 85 practised tactics and training under a new
CO, Squadron Leader Peter Townsend, in readiness for its Battle of Britain
blooding in mid-August. In a series of engagements, Frank shot down two Me
110s in one action, followed by an Me 109E, and took a share in a Dornier
17Z in subsequent combats. He was once shot down himself, baling out with a
slight foot wound, but remained with the squadron when it converted to night
operations, still piloting Hurricanes. He flew a number of fruitless missions,
seeking enemy bombers in the darkness, including the fire raid on London on
29 December 1940 that destroyed the heart of the old city. On one occasion
in the New Year, he had to force-land his Hurricane after engine failure. In
February, the squadron began re-equipping with twin-engined Douglas
Havoc night fighters as 85 continued its heavy schedule of night flying, and
in early March Walker-Smith was commissioned. On 13 March he and Flight
Lieutenant Allard were due to fly to Ford to pick up another Havoc, and Pilot

Officer Hodgson came along for the ride. A fitter was attempting to fasten a nose panel on the aircraft, and Allard, a former Halton 'brat', did the job himself. As he took off, the panel worked loose and, against all odds, flew back to jam the fighter's rudder. The Havoc flicked over on its back and crashed in a field, bursting into flames, which rapidly consumed the wreckage. Townsend later wrote of Frank that he 'was universally popular with all ranks and a very good pilot with a fine war record'. He and his companions were buried at Saffron Walden Cemetery with full military honours, and in September he was awarded a Mention in Despatches. In 1943 his Rolls-Royce colleagues placed a plaque dedicated to his memory in Spondon Church. It was unveiled by Wing Commander Harben, commandant of the Derby VR.

Frank Walker-Smith was the second Derby VR pilot to gain his flying badge after Alan Feary. He is seen here in the Highfield group photograph of 1 September 1939.

After a successful stint with 85 Squadron, Frank was killed when a Douglas Havoc night fighter, BJ500 – similar to the one shown here and piloted by Flight Lieutenant Geoffrey 'Sammy' Allard, DFC, DFM and bar, with Walker-Smith and Pilot Officer Henry Hodgson DFC as passengers – crashed on take-off from Debden on 13 March 1941.

Frank's colleagues at Rolls-Royce placed this plaque in Spondon Church in 1943. It was unveiled by Wing Commander Harben, commandant of the Derby VR.

# Sergeant Pilot
# John Primrose Wilson

'Jock' Wilson was born in Chesterfield in May 1922, of Scottish parents. His father was the township's borough engineer and surveyor, and his younger brother Bob became a noted footballer and TV sports personality. Jock won much distinction as an athlete at Chesterfield Grammar School, where he became head boy and CSM of the school Cadet Corps and developed an interest in amateur dramatics. He played rugby for Derbyshire Schools and later for teams in the RAF. With the outbreak of hostilities, he determined on a service career, which was not surprising as two of his uncles had served with the RFC and RAF in the First World War, one of them rising to the rank of air commodore with a DFC. After initial basic training, Jock commenced his flying tuition at 4 EFTS at Brough in December 1940, before a posting to 8 SFTS at Montrose. His apprenticeship concluded at 53 OTU at Heston and Llandow, and he joined 65 Squadron in July 1941. 65 operated Spitfire IIs from Kirton-in-Lindsey, and Jock was soon undertaking a full schedule of training sessions to prepare him for operational flying. During the late summer he flew a series of sweeps and escorts, before locating to 222 Squadron at North Weald in early September. 222 was equipped with Spitfire Vs, and Jock continued the busy round of escorts, convoy patrols, low-level Rhubarbs and Ramrods through the autumn and winter, occasionally strafing targets in Occupied France. On 27 February 1942 he took off with Sergeant Ralph Batman to Calais Marck Airfield, but lost his wingman when Batman had to ditch after damaging his propeller when striking a wave. Shortly afterwards Wilson was hit by flak and was killed when his Spitfire crashed. Originally buried near the crash site, his body was exhumed after the war and is buried in the Commonwealth War Grave Cemetery at Pihen-les-Guines. On 16 December 1943 his younger brother Sergeant William Primrose Wilson, an air-gunner with Bomber Command, was also reported missing. He is buried in the Reichswald Forest War Cemetery, the second sacrifice made by the grieving Wilson family.

'Jock' Wilson pictured at his Chesterfield home in 1941.

1 January 1942. Sergeant Pilot Wilson adjusts his flying helmet in this official photograph of Presentation Spitfire Vb W3253 *Central Provinces and Berar VI*, 222 Squadron.

Jock's position in this 65 Squadron line-up is indicated by a cross. He served with this unit from late July to early September 1941.

Jock then moved to 222 Squadron, and appears sitting, second from left, with his great friend 'Pat' Rusk on his right. Both pilots were killed within a month of each other in early 1942.

# Wing Commander Frank Geoffrey Woolley DFC and bar, AFC

Frank Woolley was born in Ilkeston on 1 June 1922, the son of a serving officer in the RAF who eventually reached the rank of air commodore with a CB, OBE and DFC. Frank was destined for Cranwell, but when war broke out the college closed and he went to Singapore to join his father, who taught him to fly. He was then placed with 4 AACU at Kallang in July 1940 and was posted to 4 SFTS at Habbaniya, Iraq, for further tutelage the following September. Frank was commissioned in late March 1941 and joined 244 Squadron at Shaibah near Basra, flying general-purpose Vickers Vincent biplanes. The Axis had established a pro-German government in Iraq and to protect her treaty rights, Britain invaded the country. The Iraqis responded by besieging the RAF base at Habbaniya, but the British held command of the air, forcing the enemy to retreat. With the British capture of Baghdad on 30 May 1941, the war was effectively over. On 2 May, Woolley took part in a two-plane sortie to bomb the railway line south-west of Ur to deny Iraqi forces its use, but his companion aircraft crashed, probably hit by enemy fire. Despite the rugged ground, Frank landed his Vincent and he and his gunner rescued the injured crew, despite coming under fire from Iraqi soldiers. He was awarded a DFC, although he wrote to his father stating, 'It was nothing at all. I didn't believe it when they told me.' On 26 August he was slightly wounded when his aircraft was shot down by a myopic Hurricane pilot from 261 Squadron. Frank served with 244 until April 1942, when he returned to England to train as a fighter pilot. He joined 57 OTU at Hawarden in October, gaining an 'above average' assessment, and moved to 132 Squadron at the end of January 1943, taking part in the usual fare of escorts, convoy patrols, Rodeos and Ramrods. After a Fighter Leaders' Course at Charmy Down in August he relocated to 602 Squadron AAF where operations included a spell in the Orkneys and Shetlands, and a training session at the Armament Practice Camp at Llanbedr, where the pilots practised dive and level bombing in preparation for attacks on enemy ground targets – which included launch sites for V-1 flying bombs. Following the Allied invasion, operations intensified, and on 15 June, 602 landed in France for the first time, at Bazinville ALG. Based on the Continent from 25 June, the unit carried out continuous sweeps, Frank damaging a Focke-Wulf 190D, his first combat claim. By now 'B' Flight leader, he completed his tour in early July and spent the rest of the year on the staff of the Fighter Leader School at Milfield. In early 1945 he completed a familiarisation course on the Spitfire XIV before joining 41 Squadron, part of 125 Wing, 2nd TAF at Volkel in Holland. 41 spent much time in low-level strafing attacks on German transport, although in February he claimed a probable FW 190D over Rheinie, although his own aeroplane was damaged by light flak. At the end of February Woolley was promoted to command 350 (Belgian) Squadron, and scored his first confirmed 'kill' – an FW 190D shot down in flames. In early April he was posted again as CO of 130 Squadron, based at Twente, and continued the eternal round of patrols and low-level strafing. A fellow pilot in this unit praised his squadron commander as 'unassuming … a born leader and a brilliant tactician.' In the closing days of the war Woolley added to his score with victories over an Me 108, a Seibel 204 and an FW 190A. At the end of hostilities, 130 was transferred to Fighter Command, and Frank was awarded a bar to his DFC for four enemy aircraft plus seventy-seven German vehicles destroyed. The citation recorded 'numerous hazardous missions' and Woolley's 'outstanding courage and devotion to duty on air operations'. Frank decided to make the RAF his peacetime career. He remained with 130 until July 1946, when he was granted a permanent commission as a flight lieutenant and awarded a Mention in Despatches. He was on the air staff of HQ 11 Group until December 1947, when he lost his half-stripe and became a flight commander with 54 Squadron, piloting Vampire jets. In 1948 the unit took part in a goodwill tour of Canada and the USA, an event which included the first ever crossing of the Atlantic by jet aircraft. The visit was a great success and 54 gave several outstanding flying performances in both countries. Woolley left the squadron in early 1949 and was promoted squadron leader after a course at the EFS, Hullavington. He subsequently took charge of the Bomber Command Examining Flight, followed by an Air Ministry posting and courses at the RAF Staff College and 209 AFS, Westland Zoyland. He was promoted wing commander in March 1954 and was posted to 123 Wing, Wunstorf. He was awarded the AFC in 1956. There followed three years as an instructor at the RAF Staff College before he attended a course at the RAF Flying College, Manby, in late 1959. On 28 November he took off as navigator in a Canberra B2 jet bomber en route to Malta from Strubby. The pilot lost control on take-off and ordered the other aircrew to eject. Frank cleared the aircraft, but apparently broke his arm and was unable to operate his parachute mechanism. His body was found with the unopened parachute still strapped in place. Frank was undoubtedly marked for high command, and might well, like his father before him, have achieved air rank but for his tragic end. He was cremated and his ashes were brought back to Ilkeston to lie with those of his family.

Frank Woolley as a flying officer with the DFC, Iraq, 1941.

Frank's father, Wing Commander Frank Woolley DFC, a First World War fighter pilot, served in Singapore in 1938–41. His son joined him there in 1940 and his parent taught him to fly. This picture of Swordfish torpedo bombers, probably from No. 4 AACU at Tengah, comes from Frank senior's scrapbook.

Another Malayan-based unit was 62 Squadron. One of their Blenheim Is (L1131 FX-P) was snapped by Frank senior at Kallang.

A visitor to Singapore in August 1939 was carrier HMS *Eagle*, seen here at anchor in the harbour. The warship was scheduled for a refit in the local docks, but was forced to postpone due to the threat of war.

Frank and his father pictured in Singapore in early 1940. Frank junior was then serving with No. 4 AACU.

Frank is seen here piloting Audax K3714 over the Iraqi countryside in early 1941.

A youthful Frank, by now commissioned, poses in front of an Audax at 4 SFTS Habbaniyah, Iraq, in April 1941.

Frank is standing third from left in this 132 Squadron photograph from 1943. The group pose on and around a clipped-wing Spitfire V. The fighter stands on a chain-link strip of artificial runway.

Frank, in full flying gear, in the 'office' of Presentation Spitfire LFIX MH486 (FF-F) *Ethel Marsden*, 132 Squadron, in mid-1943. The aircraft was paid for by a Lancashire mill owner, who named it after his wife.

Frank, who is standing second from left, poses with fellow pilots of 602 Squadron in front of a Spitfire IX in early 1944. Squadron Leader 'Maxie' Sutherland is fifth from left, and Pierre Clostermann eighth. The Frenchman later wrote the classic book *The Big Show*.

Flight Lieutenant
Frank Woolley
is seen here after
the presentation
of his first DFC
at Buckingham
Palace in autumn
1943.

Frank hangs on to one of the massive five blades of his Spitfire XIV's propeller at
Volkel, Holland – 41 Squadron's base in February 1945.

The massive nose and huge five-blade airscrew of Frank's Griffon-powered Spitfire XIV show up well in this view of his 350 Squadron machine *Elizabeth X* at Warmwell in March 1945.

A candid shot of Frank taken after landing from a mission in the closing days of the war.

After the war Frank remained as CO of 130 Squadron, which relinquished its Spitfire XIVs for IXs, much to the pilots' chagrin. He can be seen on the front row fifth from left in this squadron line-up, with several of the unit's aircraft in shot. The photograph was taken at Manston in late 1945.

Frank, centre, is with 130 Squadron's pilots in front of a Spitfire IX.

Frank, left, with his two flight leaders, plus squadron machines. Note the underwing links for bomb carrying.

In 1948, as a flight commander with 54 Squadron, Frank toured Canada and the USA, flying Vampire IIIs at various airshows. In this photograph he leads a section in VT869 in a virtuoso performance at Greenville, South Carolina.

# Select Bibliography

Barker, Ralph, *The Hurricats* (Pelham, 1978).

Bartley, Anthony, *Smoke Trails in the Sky* (William Kimber, 1984).

Boot, Henry & Sturtivant, Ray, *Gifts of War* (Air Britain, 2005).

Crook, David, *Spitfire Pilot* (Greenhill Books, 2006).

*Flypast* (August 2007, July 2009, July/August 2010).

Jefford, Geoffrey, *Fighter Squadrons of the RAF* (Airlife, 1988).

Marsden, Barry M., *A Few of the Derbyshire 'Few'* (KM, 1987).

Marsden, Barry M., *Derbyshire Fighter Aces of World War Two* (Tempus, 2004).

Richey, Paul, *Fighter Pilot* (Cassell, 2001).

Shores, Christopher & Williams, Clive, *Aces High* (Grub Street, 1994).